MAXnotes

Herman Melville's
Moby-Dick

Text by
Naomi Shaw
(M.A., Bridgewater State College)
Department of English
Fairhaven High School
Fairhaven, Massachusetts

Illustrations by
Karen Pica

R&E **Research & Education Association**

MAXnotes™ for
MOBY-DICK

Copyright © 1995 by Research & Education Association. All rights reserved. No part of this book may be reproduced in any form without permission of the publisher.

Printed in the United States of America

Library of Congress Catalog Card Number 95-67269

International Standard Book Number 0-87891-986-4

MAXnotes™ is a trademark of
Research & Education Association, Piscataway, New Jersey 08854

What **MAXnotes**™ *Will Do for You*

This book is intended to help you absorb the essential contents and features of Herman Melville's *Moby-Dick* and to help you gain a thorough understanding of the work. The book has been designed to do this more quickly and effectively than any other study guide.

For best results, this **MAXnotes** book should be used as a companion to the actual work, not instead of it. The interaction between the two will greatly benefit you.

To help you in your studies, this book presents the most up-to-date interpretations of every section of the actual work, followed by questions and fully explained answers that will enable you to analyze the material critically. The questions also will help you to test your understanding of the work and will prepare you for discussions and exams.

Meaningful illustrations are included to further enhance your understanding and enjoyment of the literary work. The illustrations are designed to place you into the mood and spirit of the work's settings.

The **MAXnotes** also include summaries, character lists, explanations of plot, and section-by-section analyses. A biography of the author and discussion of the work's historical context will help you put this literary piece into the proper perspective of what is taking place.

The use of this study guide will save you the hours of preparation time that would ordinarily be required to arrive at a complete grasp of this work of literature. You will be well-prepared for classroom discussions, homework, and exams. The guidelines that are included for writing papers and reports on various topics will prepare you for any added work which may be assigned.

The **MAXnotes** will take your grades "to the max."

Dr. Max Fogiel
Program Director

Contents

Section One: *Introduction* 1
    The Life and Work of Herman Melville 1
    Historical Background 2
    Master List of Characters 3
    Master List of Ships 6
    Summary of the Novel 7
    Estimated Reading Time 8

> **Each chapter includes List of Characters, Summary, Analysis, Study Questions and Answers, and Suggested Essay Topics.**

Section Two: *Moby-Dick* 9
    Chapter I 9
    Chapters II-IV 11
    Chapters V-IX 15
    Chapters X-XV 19
    Chapters XVI-XVIII 22
    Chapters XIX-XXV 26
    Chapters XXVI-XXXI 29
    Chapters XXXII-XXXV 33

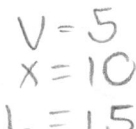

Chapters XXXVI-XL 37
Chapters XLI-XLII 41
Chapters XLIII-XLVII 44
Chapters XLVIII-LI 47
Chapters LII-LIV 51
Chapters LV-LX 55
Chapters LXI-LXVI 57
Chapters LXVII-LXXI 61
Chapters LXXII-LXXVIII 65
Chapters LXXIX-LXXXI 69
Chapters LXXXII-LXXXVI 72
Chapters LXXXVII-XCII 74
Chapters XCIII-XCIX 78
Chapters C-CV 81
Chapters CVI-CIX 84
Chapters CX-CXIV 86
Chapters CXV-CXXI 90
Chapters CXXII-CXXVII 94
Chapters CXXVIII-CXXXII 96
Chapters CXXXIII-CXXXV and Epilogue 101

Section Three: *Sample Analytical Paper Topics* 106

Section Four: *Bibliography* 110

SECTION ONE

Introduction

The Life and Work of Herman Melville

Melville dedicated *Moby-Dick* to Nathaniel Hawthorne "in admiration for his genius." The two met in 1850 when Melville moved from New York to Pittsfield, Massachusetts. For a time, Melville and his family lived on a 160-acre farm called Arrowhead, where he finished the writing of *Moby-Dick* in 1851.

Moby-Dick, like many of Melville's other sea stories, is based on life experience. In 1819, Melville was born in New York City to Allan Melvill (the final "e" was added to the name later) and Maria Gansevoort. When the family business failed and Allan Melvill died in 1832, Herman left the Albany Academy and joined his older brother in a futile attempt to restore the family fortune. In 1839, Melville signed onto a British ship, the *St. Lawrence,* which was sailing to Liverpool.

Two years later he signed aboard the *Achushnet,* a whaler bound for the South Seas. Misery and brutality drove Melville and a companion to desert the ship in the Marquesas Islands. In June of 1842, the two sailors lived with the Typees for a short time. Fearing that the Typees were cannibals, Melville escaped to the *Lucy Ann*, another whaler, but it proved even worse than the *Acushnet.* He abandoned this ship in Tahiti. His one successful whaling voyage was aboard the *Charles and Henry.* In 1844, Melville left the sea after a year's service aboard the naval vessel *United States.*

All of these sea adventures provided material for Melville's writing. *Typee* (1846), *Omoo* (1847), *Redburn* (1848), and *White-Jacket* (1850) chronicle his experiences among the natives and aboard ships. These works also expose the ill treatment of sailors and natives.

Three years after Melville gave up the life of a sailor, he married Elizabeth Shaw, daughter of Judge Lemuel Shaw, chief justice of Massachusetts. In 1849, their first son, Malcolm, was born. To restore the family's finances, Melville hurriedly wrote *Redburn* and *White-Jacket*. He traveled to Europe shortly after and returned to join the family in their New York City home in 1850.

It was at this time that Melville began writing *Moby-Dick*, "a romance of adventure, founded upon certain wild legends in the Southern Sperm Whale Fisheries, and illustrated by the author's own personal experiences." After the publication of *Moby-Dick*, the author produced *Pierre* (1852) and several shorter works including "Bartleby the Scrivener" (1852) and "Benito Cereno" (1855). Melville published his Civil War poems in 1866 and was appointed customs inspector for the port of New York.

Melville's later years were marked by illness and depression. During this period, Melville wrote *Billy Budd, Sailor*, which was published posthumously. Melville died on September 28, 1891. He is buried in New York's Woodlawn Cemetery.

Historical Background

The spirit of adventure and rugged individualism evident in Melville's work was the spirit of the age in which he lived. The Manifest Destiny doctrine defined the country's will to grow and spread its democracy throughout the hemisphere. Westward expansion accelerated after the economic depression of 1837, and American pioneers conquered the frontier.

At the same time, New England whaling captains and their crews were conquering the great fishing grounds throughout the world. New Bedford, Massachusetts, the setting of the opening scene in *Moby-Dick*, had a fleet of over 300 whaling ships. Melville himself sailed from this port on the *Acushnet* in 1841.

The mid-nineteenth century was not only a period of geographic growth, but also a time of ideological growth. The innate worth of all humanity, an idea developed in *Moby-Dick* was the concept at the heart of the slavery debate. As new territories were admitted to the union, the question of slavery became a national concern. In the 1850s, the activities of the abolitionists, the publication of *Uncle Tom's Cabin*, and the Fugitive Slave Law fomented heated debate and controversy.

Ralph Waldo Emerson and transcendentalism dominated the intellectual scene mid-century. In *Moby-Dick* ,the theme of the interconnectedness of all things in the universe reflects transcendental thought. Hawthorne, to whom *Moby-Dick* was dedicated, Thoreau, Poe, and Walt Whitman dominated the literary scene of that time. These writers, along with Melville, produced a body of work distinctly American.

Ironically, *Moby-Dick*, one of the greatest works of American literature, was not recognized as such at the time of its publication. Reviews ranged from ardent praise to hostile attack; from "surpasses any of the former productions of this highly successful author" to "trash belonging to the worst of the Bedlam school of literature" (*Criticism and Context*, 544, 546). One critic commented that the book would be "flung aside" by the common reader (*Criticism and Context*, 546). His prediction was accurate, for *Moby-Dick* sold fewer than 3,000 copies (McSweeney, 18). It was not until the late 1930s that *Moby-Dick* became part of the American literary canon.

Master List of Characters

Ahab—*the monomaniacal, peg-legged captain of the* Pequod *Old Thunder is determined to destroy Moby-Dick at any cost.*

Archy—*a sailor aboard the* Pequod; *he hears noises from afterhold and suspects someone is being kept down there.*

Aunt Charity—*Captain Bildad's sister; she is a kind old lady who substituted ginger water for grog aboard the* Pequod

Bildad—*a Nantucketer, Quaker, and part owner of the* Pequod; *he signs on Ishmael and Queequeg.*

Bulkington—*the helmsman; having just returned from one voyage, he sails again on* Pequod *and dies at sea.*

Bumpkin—*young rascal who makes fun of Queequeg on schooner from New Bedford to Nantucket; he is later rescued by Queequeg.*

Cabaco—*a* Pequod *sailor who scoffs at Archy's suspicions that someone is hidden below deck.*

Captain Boomer—*the good-natured captain of the* Samuel Enderby; *he lost arm to Moby Dick, and warns Ahab to give up his hunt.*

Captain Gardiner—*the captain of the* Rachel; *he is a Nantucketer known to Ahab, and begs Ahab's help in finding his lost son.*

Captain Mayhew—*the captain of the* Jeroboam *of Nantucket; his ship has an epidemic aboard.*

Captain of the *Albatross*—*asked if he has seen Moby Dick,; his answer is lost when he drops his megaphone into the sea.*

Captain of the *Bachelor*—*he invites Ahab to join him and his crew in celebrating their journey home.*

Captain of the *Delight*—*he lost five men to Moby Dick and tells Ahab no harpoon can kill the White Whale.*

Carpenter—*he makes Queequeg's coffin and then caulks it to make it a life buoy.; he makes a new leg for Ahab.*

Daggoo—*an "imperial, coal-black Negro"; he is a harpooner for Flask.*

Derrick De Deer—*captain of the* Jungfrau *whose ship is out of oil; he loses a contest with the* Pequod *to catch a whale.*

Dr. Bunger—*gives Ahab details of Captain Boomer's wound.*

Dons Pedro and Sebastian—*Spanish friends of Ishmael to whom he told the story of the* Town-Ho.

Dough-Boy—Pequod's *steward; he is nervous, "bread-faced."*

Elijah—*a ragged "prophet" who stops Ishmael and Queequeg; he dismays Ishmael with his vague warnings about Ahab.*

Father Mapple—*a former harpooner who is the minister of the Whaleman's Chapel in New Bedford; he gives a sermon about Jonah.*

Fedallah—*the Parsee, a mysterious harpooner for Ahab's boat; he*

Introduction

interprets Ahab's dream and dies lashed to Moby Dick.

Flask—*the third mate; called King-Post for his stout figure and stalwartness, he has little fear of or respect for whales.*

Fleece—*an old, arch-backed Negro cook.; he cooks Stubb's whale steak and delivers a sermon to the sharks.*

Gabriel—*the crazed "prophet" of the Jeroboam; he calls Moby Dick a Shaker god and warns against attacking him.*

Guernsey-man—*chief mate of the Rose-Bud; with Stubb's help he gets his captain to cut rotting whale carcasses free.*

Hosea and Mrs. Hussey—*owners of the Try Pots Inn of Nantucket where Ishmael and Queequeg stay and eat chowder.*

Ishmael—*narrator of the story; he survives by clinging to Queequeg's floating coffin.*

Macey—*the former chief mate of the Jeroboam who was killed by Moby Dick; the Pequod tries to deliver a letter to him.*

Manxman—*an old Pequod sailor from the Isle of Man; he warns Ahab that the line holding the log will not hold.*

Moby Dick—*a sperm whale, "white-headed with a wrinkled brow and a crooked jaw"; god, devil, or dumb brute; he destroys Ahab.*

Peleg—*a Nantucketer, Quaker, and part owner of the Pequod; he is impressed by Queequeg's skill as a harpooner.*

Perth—*a "begrimed, blistered old blacksmith"; he forges Ahab's harpoon which is tempered in blood.*

Peter Coffin—*landlord of the Spouter Inn in New Bedford; he gives Ishmael a bed to share with Queequeg.*

Pip—*a little black "ship-keeper" who goes mad after being left in the water; Ahab becomes attached to him.*

Queequeg—*a harpooner who is a devoted friend of Ishmael. He is a tattooed savage of noble birth; saves Tashtego.*

Radney—*the former mate of the Town-Ho; he is an enemy of Steelkilt, and is devoured by Moby Dick.*

Starbuck—*the chief mate of the Pequod.; he opposes Ahab and tries* to convince him to give up his quest.

Steelkilt—*a mutineer on the Town-Ho; he is about to murder Radney when Moby Dick interrupts the plan.*

Stubb—*Pequod's "good humored" second mate.; he kills the first whale and leaves Pip in the water expecting him to be picked up.*

Tashtego—*an American Indian, harpooner for Stubb; he falls into the tun of a whale but is saved.*

Yojo—*Queequeg's "black little god" to whom he prays and from whom he obtains guidance.*

Master List of Ships

The *Albatross*—*her captain drops his megaphone; so the* Pequod *is unable to communicate with her.*

The *Bachelor*—*a homeward bound ship celebrating a very profitable voyage.*

The *Delight*—*a whaler that lost five men to Moby Dick; she is in the process of burying one at sea when the* Pequod *approaches.*

The *Jeroboam*—*a whaler that has an epidemic on board; the crazed Gabriel is one of her crew.*

The *Jungfrau*—*called* Virgin *in German, her captain asked the* Pequod *for oil; she competed with the* Pequod *for a whale and lost.*

The *Rachel*—*a Nantucket whaler whose captain was searching for his son lost in a chase for Moby Dick; she picks up Ishmael after the* Pequod *sinks.*

The *Rose-Bud*—*an odoriferous ship with two rotting whales lashed along her side, tricked by Stubb.*

The *Samuel Enderby*—*an English ship whose captain had lost an arm to Moby Dick.*

The *Town-Ho*—*manned by Polynesians; the first mate, Radney, is killed by Moby Dick; the ship is deserted by Steelkilt and the crew.*

Introduction

Summary of the Novel

Ishmael, the narrator of the story, explains that he goes to sea whenever he is depressed. In the port of New Bedford, he stays at the Spouter Inn. He is at first frightened by Queequeg, his tattooed, tomahawk-toting bedmate, who has been out selling shrunken heads. Queequeg soon becomes Ishmael's bosom friend.

Ishmael attends a service at the Whaleman's Chapel where Father Mapple gives a sermon about Jonah and the whale. The next day, Queequeg and Ishmael set out for Nantucket where they sign onto a whaler. On the ferry ride to the island, a young man mocks Queequeg. Later, this same young man falls overboard and is saved by Queequeg.

While Queequeg performs his rites of Ramadan in the room at the Try Pots, Ishmael signs onto the whaler *Pequod* owned by the Quaker captains, Bildad and Peleg. The heathen Queequeg must prove his skill as a harpooner before he is accepted.

As the two friends are about to board the *Pequod*, they are accosted by the crazed Elijah, who utters vague warnings about Ahab and the voyage. In the mist, they see four or five shadowy figures go aboard. The ship sets sail on Christmas day. The chief mate, Starbuck, chooses Queequeg for his harpooneer; the second mate, Stubb, chooses the Indian, Tashtego; and the third mate, Flask, chooses the African, Daggoo.

Several days after the ship sets sail, Ahab finally appears on deck. His appearance sends shivers through Ishmael. A white scar runs from his hairline, over his face, and down his neck beneath his clothing. He stands upon an artificial leg made of whale bone.

Ahab calls all men on deck. He hammers a gold doubloon to the mast and tells the men that the first to spot Moby Dick, the white whale, will win the coin. Ahab admits that it was Moby Dick that took off his leg.

When the first whale is sighted and the boats are lowered, the sailors are surprised to see Ahab in his own boat with a mysterious crew who had been hidden below deck. The exotic Fedallah is his harpooner. A squall comes up during the chase. Ishmael's boat capsizes and is later nearly rammed by the *Pequod*.

After rounding the Cape of Good Hope, the ship has its first of many gams, or meetings with other ships. Ahab's sole purpose in communicating with these ships is to get news of Moby Dick. Several of the ships have lost men to the whale. The *Rachel* has recently chased Moby Dick and is now searching for a lost boat. The young son of the captain is in that boat, but Ahab refuses to join the search. Starbuck confronts Ahab and tries to convince him to abandon his mission to get his revenge on Moby Dick.

Stubb's boat is the first to kill a whale. While Stubb eats his whale steak, Fleece, the cook, delivers a sermon to the sharks. During the cleaning of another whale, Tashtego falls into the tun, the forehead of the whale containing the spermaceti. When the head breaks loose from the ship and falls into the water, Tashtego is rescued by Queegueg. Pip, the timid black boy, is temporarily abandoned in the sea during another whale chase which drives him to madness. Queequeg, stricken with fever and believing death is near, has the ship's carpenter build him a coffin.

Ahab has the blacksmith fashion a special harpoon, tempered in the blood of the heathen harpooners. During a storm, Ahab holds the harpoon above his head and it is struck by lightning. Later, Ahab has a dream, which is interpreted by Fedallah. The Parsee predicts that he will die before Ahab, that only hemp can kill Ahab, and that before he dies, Ahab will see two hearses upon the sea.

At last, Moby Dick is sighted by Ahab. The chase lasts three days. Fedallah dies, lashed by tangled lines to the body of the great beast. Ahab thrusts his harpoon into Moby Dick, but his line runs afoul and catches him around the neck; he is pulled down to the depths. Moby Dick smashes into the bow of the *Pequod*, and Queequeg's coffin shoots out of the whirlpool created by the sinking ship. The only survivor, Ishmael, clings to this strange life buoy and is later rescued.

Estimated Reading Time

Reading time will improve as the reader becomes accustomed to Melville's style. In an hour's sitting, 30 to 35 pages could be covered. The book could be completed in 20 to 25 hours.

SECTION TWO

Moby-Dick

Chapter I

New Character:

Ishmael: *the narrator of the story; a seaman*

Summary

Ishmael explains he has chosen to go to sea to cure his depression as an alternative to suicide. There is "magic" in bodies of water, he says. "Crowds of water-gazers" flock to the wharfs of Manhattan, a temporary escape from the occupations in which they are "pent up." Wanderers in the woods find their way to lakes.

Ishmael never goes to sea as a passenger; he doesn't have the money to pay. He never goes as an officer; he has all he can do to take care of himself. He never goes as a cook. Rather, he goes to sea as a "simple sailor" to get paid, to get exercise, and to breathe the pure air. He overcomes the indignity of being ordered around since he believes that everyone else is a slave in one way or another.

Although he may delude himself into believing his choice is his own, it is fate that sends Ishmael on a whaling voyage. His chief motives are the mystery of the whale itself and the marvels of the seas he will sail.

Analysis

"Call me Ishmael" is undoubtedly one of the most famous opening lines in all of literature. The name is an allusion to the biblical character who was cast out of Abraham's household, set adrift as it were. The title of the chapter, "Loomings," meaning an ominous event about to occur, establishes a sense of foreboding.

At the outset, in analyzing his own motives, the narrator shows himself to be open-minded, philosophical, and observant. His journey is nothing less than a quest for knowledge and understanding: the sea, or perhaps Ishmael's own reflection in it, is "the ungraspable phantom of life; ...the key to it all." The ocean as a central symbol is introduced in this chapter. The water offers not only freedom from a mundane existence, but also freedom of thought.

The first chapter is written in an ironic, humorous tone. Ishmael's depression is serious and borders on self-destruction, but it is described in such understated terms as "pausing before coffin warehouses" and "bringing up the rear of every funeral." Ishmael humorously describes God's plan for him as a warm-up act sandwiched between "more extensive performances." There is a good deal of irony and humor in *Moby-Dick* that must not be overlooked.

Study Questions

1. Explain the biblical allusion to Ishmael.
2. What does Ishmael do whenever he finds himself growing "grim about the mouth"?
3. What does Ishmael mean by a "substitute for pistol and ball"?
4. What proof does Ishmael offer that others feel the same as he does about the sea?
5. What is some of the "magic" which water performs for men?
6. How did the Greeks and the Persians perceive the sea?
7. How did Narcissus die?
8. Other than not having the money, why does Ishmael never go to sea as a passenger?
9. How does Ishmael explain his willingness to be ordered around?
10. What are Ishmael's chief motives in going whaling?

Answers

1. The biblical Ishmael was banished by Abraham. Melville's Ishmael is also set adrift.
2. Ishmael goes to sea.
3. Going to sea is the substitute for "pistol and ball," by which he means shooting himself.
4. "Leagues" of people from all over are drawn to the shore and need to get as close to the water as they can.
5. Water puts men into states of reverie and unites them. It draws them into deep thought.
6. The Persians saw the sea as being holy; the Greeks saw it as powerful enough to have its own god.
7. Narcissus drowned when he plunged toward his reflection in the water.
8. They get sick, can't sleep, and don't enjoy themselves.
9. Ishmael says that in the grand scheme of things we are all "thumped" around either physically or mentally.
10. The idea of the whale is Ishmael's chief motive.

Suggested Essay Topics

1. Prove that Ishmael is an analytical, philosophical thinker by examining his reasons for going to sea. Give special attention to the reason he gives as his primary motive.
2. Discuss the biblical and classical allusions employed in Chapter I. Thoroughly explain each allusion and discuss its thematic implications.

Chapters II – IV

New Characters:

Peter Coffin: *the owner of the Spouter Inn*

Bulkington: *a whaler in the Spouter Inn just returned from a voyage*

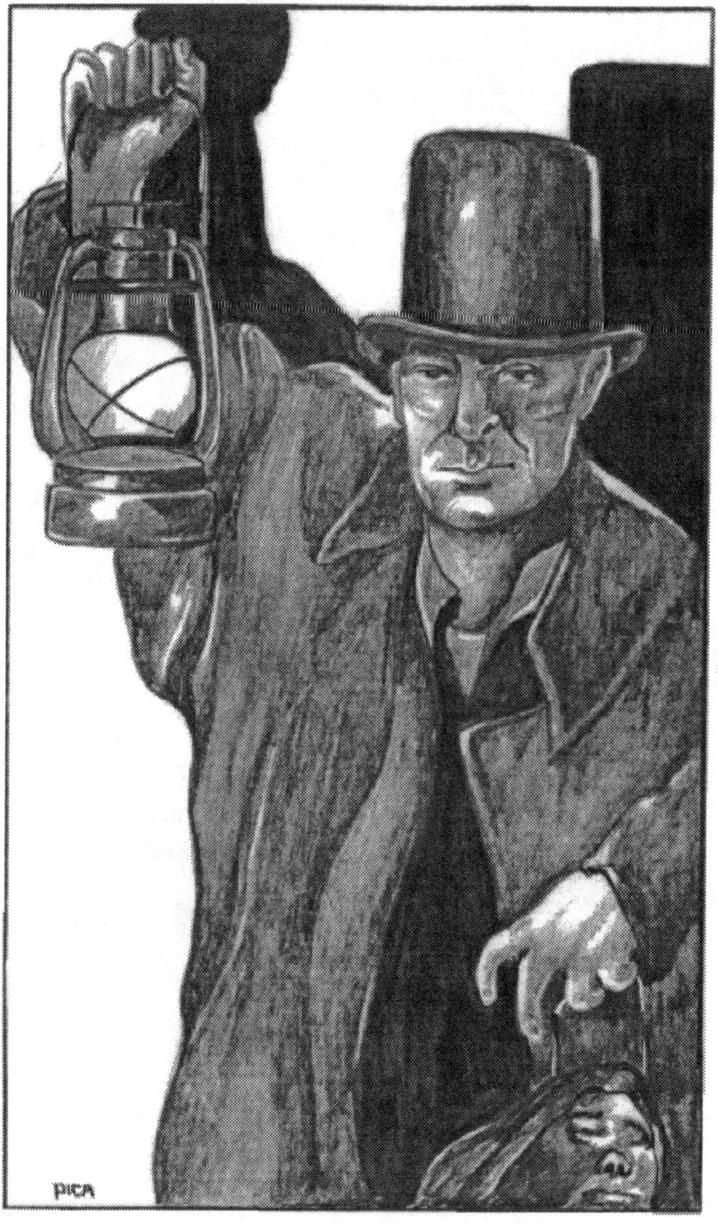
PICA

Chapters II-IV

Queequeg: *a pagan harpooner with whom Ishmael must share a bed*

Summary

Ishmael stays over in New Bedford, waiting for a packet to take him to Nantucket. He searches the cold, dark streets for a place to stay. After accidentally going into a "Negro church," he comes upon a sign, "The Spouter Inn:—Peter Coffin."

The entryway of the inn reminds Ishmael of a "condemned old craft." Dominating the scene is a large, enigmatic oil painting, which Ishmael interprets as a "half-foundered" ship in a hurricane with a whale leaping up as if to impale himself on the masts. Peter Coffin tells Ishmael that he must share a bed with a harpooner. Ishmael observes the activities of the inn, taking special interest in a tall, silent man named Bulkington. He will soon be Ishmael's shipmate in spite of the fact that he has just returned from a voyage.

Ishmael grows fearful of sharing a bed with a stranger and tries unsuccessfully to sleep on a bench. He opts for the bed even after Peter Coffin tells him that this harpooner is off peddling a shrunken head. Ishmael is in bed when the dark stranger enters. His head is bald except for a small scalp-knot, and he is tattooed all over. He removes an ebony idol from his bag, performs a sort of prayer, and smokes his tomahawk pipe, which he brings to bed with him. Ishmael screams for the landlord who assures him that Queequeg will do him no harm. Ishmael sleeps soundly.

He wakes with Queequeg's arm thrown over him. With some difficulty, Ishmael awakens his bedfellow. Queequeg dresses in his tall beaver hat and crawls under the bed to put on his boots. He shaves with his harpoon.

Analysis

Melville uses the doubling technique, bringing opposites together to create contrasts. For example, although the tone of this section is light, much of the imagery is dark and foreboding. The tone is amusing as Ishmael walks along talking to himself, telling himself that the Sword-Fish Inn is much too jolly and expensive.

His misunderstanding of Peter Coffin's meaning when he tells Ishmael that Queequeg is out selling his head is verbal comedy of the "who's on first" variety. And the bedroom scene provides terrific physical comedy.

On the other hand, the atmosphere is dismal. The New Bedford streets are icy and dark. The light in a house looks like a candle in a tomb. A box of ashes reminds Ishmael of the biblical city of Gomorrah destroyed by God for its evil. The Spouter Inn is owned by a man named Coffin; its entryway is described in terms of the direful painting and the instruments of death hanging on its walls. Ishmael contemplates his own vulnerability in a hostile universe when he compares himself to a house whose chinks and crannies have not been stopped up. The cold wind blows through, and "Death is the only glazier."

Likewise, the budding friendship of Ishmael and Queequeg is the bringing together of opposites. Ishmael, the civilized Christian, learns tolerance from his pagan friend. Early in the bedroom scene, Ishmael reminds himself that "ignorance is the parent of fear." In fact, Ishmael admits, "(Queequeg) treated me with so much civility and consideration, while I was guilty of great rudeness." Ishmael's comment that "naught but death" would part him and Queequeg foreshadows events to follow.

Study Questions

1. Why does Ishmael not stay at the Sword-Fish Inn?
2. Who owns the Spouter Inn?
3. What is in the painting in the entry of the inn?
4. What is the name of the old man who tends the bar?
5. Where is Ishmael's bedmate early in the evening?
6. Where does Ishmael try to sleep at first?
7. What is odd about Queequeg's appearance?
8. What did Queequeg do with his ebony idol?
9. What did Queequeg take into bed with him?
10. How did Queequeg shave?

Answers

1. The Sword-Fish Inn was too jolly and too expensive.
2. Peter Coffin owns the inn.
3. The painting is of a sinking ship and of a whale leaping over it, impaling itself on the masts.
4. Jonah is the name of the old man who tends the bar.
5. He is out selling a shrunken head.
6. Ishmael tries to sleep on a wooden bench.
7. Queequeg is tattooed all over, and his head is shaved all except for a skull-knot of hair.
8. Queequeg set his idol before the fire and made an offering to it.
9. Queequeg took his tomahawk pipe into the bed.
10. Queequeg shaved with the blade of his harpoon.

Suggested Essay Topics

1. Explain how Melville uses the doubling technique in characterization. How are Ishmael and Queequeg different? How are they brought together? How does Queequeg's appearance compare to his behavior?
2. Describe the setting of this section and tell how it contrasts with tone. Give specific details of the streets, the inn, the bar, and the bedroom. What tone does Melville use in this section? How does he achieve that tone?

Chapters V – IX

New Character:

Father Mapple: *pastor of the seamen's chapel*

Summary

Ishmael greets his landlord and bears no hard feelings for the

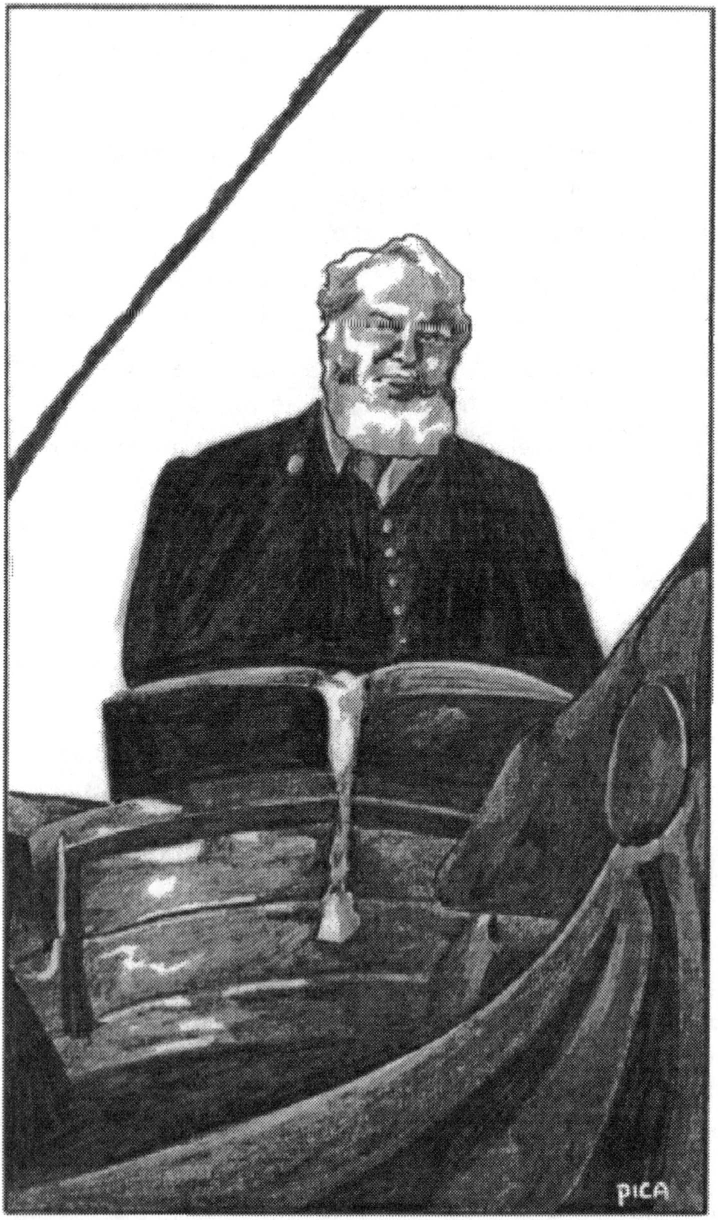
PICA

joke Peter Coffin played in the matter of his bedfellow. All the boarders, mostly whalemen, gather at the table for breakfast. Although they are all adventurers, paradoxically, they are timid in the social setting. Queequeg sits at the head of the table, using his harpoon to "grapple" the steak.

After breakfast, Ishmael ventures into the streets of New Bedford where he sees all manner of people including "cannibals chatting at street corners" and hayseeds from Vermont "athirst for the glory" of whaling. Nonetheless, New Bedford is "the dearest place to live" with its lovely parks, gardens, and patrician houses all gotten from the bounty of the sea.

He stops into the Whaleman's Chapel. The walls are lined with marble tablets put up in memory of those who have lost their lives to whaling. Queequeg is there. Father Mapple mounts the pulpit by way of a ship's ladder which he draws up after him. The pulpit itself is a ship's prow.

The sermon is based on the story of Jonah, who had been commanded by God to go to a foreign land to preach. He disobeyed God and was punished by being swallowed by a whale. He repented and was saved.

Analysis

Ishmael bears no grudge against Peter Coffin for he values good humor. "A good laugh is a mighty good thing...And the man that has anything bountifully laughable about him, be sure there is more in that man than you perhaps think." This principle might be applied not only to Ishmael but also to the author, who chooses to employ humor.

The theme of death begins to be developed more significantly in this section. In the chapel, the marble tablets lead Ishmael to consider the resurrection of those without graves. He wonders why people mourn for dead ones who in the afterlife supposedly dwell in bliss. In a striking simile, faith is compared to a jackal that "feeds among the tombs...and even from these dead doubts" gathers "her most vital hope."

Ishmael grows "merry" as he thinks of death as a sort of promotion that his whaling voyage might offer him. He describes death as "a speechlessly quick bundling of a man into eternity." After all, his soul, not his body, is his true substance. The bringing together of opposites in previous chapters continues here as Melville focuses on the dual nature of man, the spiritual and the physical.

The theme of isolation is introduced in this section. The pulpit isolates Father Mapple and "signifies his spiritual withdrawal …from the outward worldly ties." Similarly, Ishmael's metaphoric journey for understanding must bring him into the realm of the spiritual, away from worldly ties. Frequently in literature, a water voyage is a symbolic separation from previously unquestioned beliefs. It is a venture into a fluid realm where there are no absolutes; yet many find enlightenment there.

Father Mapple's sermon is about not only sin and redemption, but also "Gospel duty…to preach the truth to the face of falsehood." In a metaphor, Ishmael compares the world to a ship and the pulpit to its prow. Ishmael is fulfilling his Gospel through the telling of this story.

Study Questions

1. Why does Ishmael not begrudge the joke played on him by Peter Coffin?
2. What is the purpose of the marble tablets in the chapel?
3. Who sat near Ishmael in the chapel?
4. What was Father Mapple's previous occupation?
5. Describe the pulpit.
6. How did Father Mapple get to it?
7. What biblical character is the subject of the sermon?
8. What was his sin?
9. What happened to him when he was cast into the sea?
10. In what way does Ishmael fulfill his Gospel duty?

Answers

1. Ishmael knows the value of good humor, that beneath it is something deeper.
2. The tablets memorialize those lost at sea.

3. Queequeg sat near Ishmael.
4. Father Mapple had been a harpooner.
5. The pulpit is a ship's prow raised high above the congregation.
6. Father Mapple climbed a ship's ladder to get to the pulpit.
7. Jonah is the subject of the sermon.
8. Willful disobedience was his sin.
9. He was swallowed by a whale.
10. Ishmael fulfills his Gospel duty by telling this story.

Suggested Essay Topics

1. Compare Ishmael's morbid thoughts upon entering the chapel to his more positive thoughts about death.
2. Discuss the theme of isolation as it relates to Father Mapple, Jonah, and Ishmael.

Chapters X – XV

New Characters:

Bumpkin: *mocks Queequeg on packet to Nantucket*

Mr. and Mrs. Hosea Hussey: *owners of the Try Pots Inn*

Summary

Ishmael returns to the Spouter Inn, where he finds Queequeg turning through the pages of a book. They share a smoke from the tomahawk pipe, and Queequeg declares Ishmael a bosom friend for whom he would die. Ishmael joins Queequeg in his rites of praising the ebony idol.

Queequeg tells Ishmael of his past. The son of a high chief from Kokovoko, Queequeg was determined to learn more about Christians and to bring his knowledge back to his people to make them happier. After being picked up by a ship, he discovered that Christians have little to offer his people.

The two friends use a wheelbarrow to bring their belongings aboard *The Moss*, the Nantucket packet. A "bumpkin" makes fun of Queequeg, who deftly tosses him into the air. While the captain berates Queequeg, the boom flies loose and knocks the bumpkin overboard. Queequeg dives in and saves him. Arriving at the Try Pots Inn, the two sailors are served clam and fish chowders by Mrs. Hussey.

Analysis

Ishmael's first major step in both his literal and symbolic journey begins with his acceptance of Queequeg as his bosom friend. "You cannot hide the soul," he says as he penetrates Queequeg's outlandish exterior to recognize the noble being within. Ishmael feels a "melting" away of false beliefs. " ...How elastic our stiff prejudices grow when love once comes to bend them." His participating in Queequeg's ritual worship of the idol suggests an essential unity in the spirituality of human beings. The "magnanimous God of heaven and earth" is the God of "pagans and all."

The significance of the bringing together of opposites becomes clear in this section. From what appears to be an insignificant observation about feeling cozy and warm, Ishmael draws an important truth. " ...Truly to enjoy bodily warmth, some small part of you must be cold, for there is no quality in this world that is not what it is merely by contrast. Nothing exists in itself." Duality, then, the tension of contrasts, is the very nature of existence.

Queequeg proves Ishmael's assessment of him to be true. His biography shows his fearless and benevolent nature. His saving of the bumpkin shows his bravery, selflessness, and willingness to forgive. It is no wonder that Ishmael decides to cleave to Queequeg "like a barnacle."

Ishmael has learned, "It's a mutual, joint-stock world", where cannibals may help Christians. He has learned that cultural differences are insignificant. The wheelbarrow analogy illustrates the point. People laughed at Queequeg when he filled a wheelbarrow and then carried the whole lot on his shoulder. People of Queequeg's land laughed at the captain who washed his hands in what was really a punch bowl.

Chapters X-XV

The section contains a good deal of foreshadowing. Ishmael refers to Queequeg's "last long dive." The old top mast from which the Try Pots' sign is suspended reminds him of a two-sided gallows. Ishmael feels a sense of foreboding.

The ominous mood once again is relieved by humor. When Mrs. Hussey poses the question, "Clam or cod?" Ishmael believes he will be served a single clam for supper. He also wonders if eating chowder will make him a "chowder head."

Study Questions

1. What does Queequeg share with Ishmael?
2. What pledge does Queequeg make to Ishmael?
3. What gift does Queequeg give Ishmael?
4. How does Ishmael show his friendship to Queequeg?
5. Where is Queequeg from?
6. For what purpose did Queequeg leave his native land?
7. What had Queequeg mistakenly carried on his shoulders?
8. Where do Queequeg and Ishmael go to sign onto a whaler?
9. Who insults Queequeg on the ferry ride?
10. Whom does Queequeg save from drowning?

Answers

1. Queequeg shares his pipe with Ishmael.
2. Queequeg would sacrifice his own life for Ishmael.
3. Queequeg gives Ishmael a shrunken head.
4. Ishmael joins Queequeg in his worship of the idol.
5. Queequeg is from Kokovoko.
6. Queequeg wanted to make his people happier by bringing Christian ways back to them.
7. Queequeg carried a full wheelbarrow on his shoulders.
8. Queequeg and Ishmael go to Nantucket to sign onto a whaler.

9. A bumpkin mocks Queequeg.
10. Queequeg saves the bumpkin from drowning.

Suggested Essay Topics
1. Explain the analogy of the wheelbarrow and the punch. What point was Queequeg illustrating? What proof do we have that Ishmael has learned this lesson already?
2. List four adjectives that describe Queequeg. Support your choices by explaining what he says and does.

Chapters XVI – XVIII

New Characters:

Yojo: *Queequeg's little god, the black idol*

Captains Peleg and Bildad: *Quaker Nantucketers, owners of the* Pequod

Captain Ahab: *captain of the* Pequod

The *Pequod*: *ship onto which Ishmael signs*

Summary

Queequeg believes that Yojo has told him to have Ishmael pick out a whaling ship. While Queequeg begins his day of fasting, Ishmael chooses the *Pequod*. He signs on with the owners, Bildad and Peleg, who after some bickering, give Ishmael the 300th lay, his share of the profit from the whaling voyage.

When Ishmael asks to see his captain, Peleg tells him Ahab is at home, neither sick nor well. Ishmael learns that Ahab lost his leg to a whale and that he has a wife and child. Peleg alludes to a typhoon during which he and Ahab saved the *Pequod* and her men.

When Ishmael returns to his room, he finds it locked. Concerned for Queequeg, he breaks down the door to find his friend squatting silently in the middle of the room, Yojo on his head. At sunup, Queequeg's ritual ends.

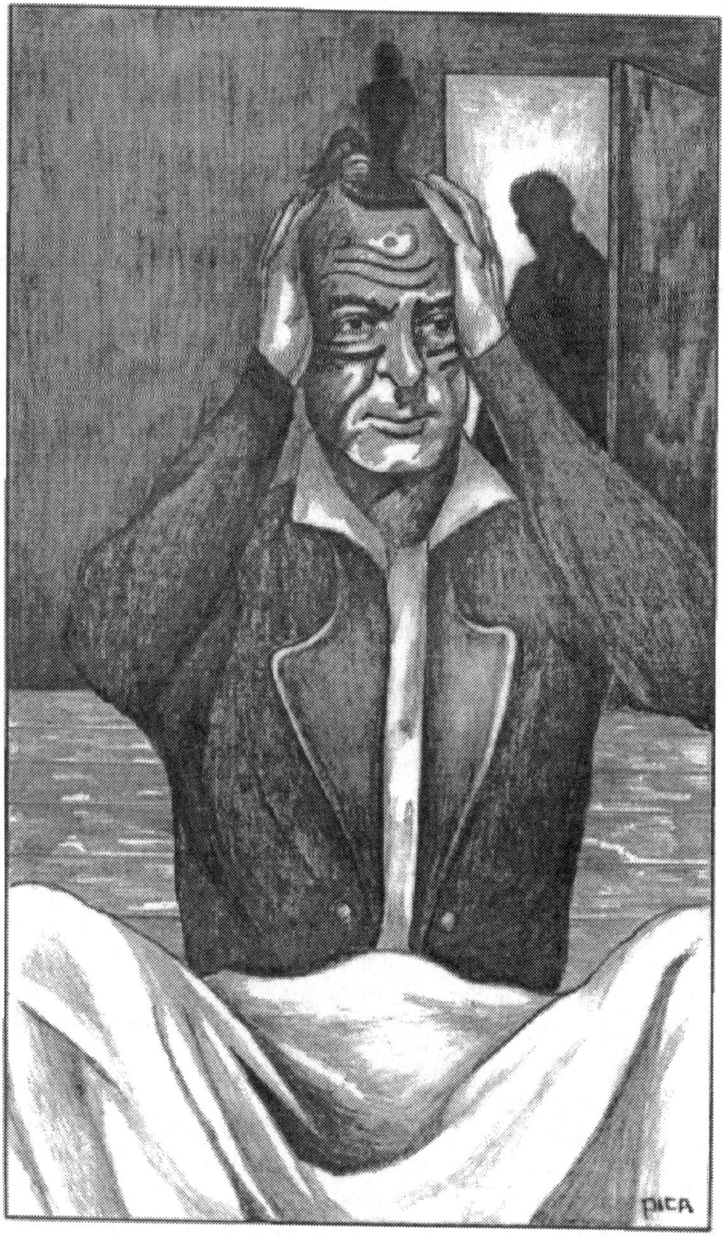
pica

Bildad and Peleg are reluctant to sign a heathen onto the *Pequod*. Queequeg proves his skill as a harpooner by hitting a small spot of tar on the water. Peleg signs him on under the name of Quohog, beneath which Queequeg makes his mark, the symbol tattooed on his arm.

Analysis

The question of the role of fate is raised once again in this section. Queequeg believes Yojo has chosen the vessel for him and his friend and that Ishmael is fated to choose that particular vessel.

Ishmael's ambiguous feelings about religion become more apparent. His tolerance of Queequeg's worship weakens as he tries to dissuade him from fasting. " ...All these Lents, Ramadans were stark nonsense; bad for the health; useless for the soul." Ishmael's remark that he has "the greatest respect for everybody's religious obligations, never mind how comical," proves that in fact he has yet to feel the respect he professes. Nonetheless, he convinces the two Quakers that Queequeg, like everyone, belongs to "the great and everlasting First Congregation of this whole worshipping world."

The beliefs and practices of the Quaker Bildad raise more questions about religion. Bildad "had the reputation of being an incorrigible old hunk, and in his sea-going days, a bitter, hard task-master." In all appearances the most pious of men, Bildad is in reality "hardhearted."

Images associated with the *Pequod* foreshadow death. The vessel is named after an extinct Indian tribe. Her decks are compared to the flagstones of Canterbury Cathedral where "Becket bled," a reference to the assassination of the archbishop by the men of Henry II. Her winches are made from whales' teeth; her tiller from the jaw. "A noble craft, but somehow a most melancholy! All noble things are touched with that."

Peleg's description of Ahab is similarly paradoxical. We see at once his dualistic nature, a man of contradictions. "He's a grand, ungodly, god-like man." Although his biblical namesake was a crowned king, he was a "very vile one." He's like any average man, but "there's a good deal more to him." He's "moody" and "savage," but "Ahab has his humanities." Ishmael feels both pity and awe for

Ahab. This introduction suggests that Ahab is a likely tragic hero.

Study Questions

1. What is the name of Queequeg's idol?
2. What had the little god told Queequeg?
3. After what is the *Pequod* named?
4. What are her winches and tiller made out of?
5. Who are the owners of the *Pequod*?
6. What had the old squaw Tistig said of Ahab?
7. What does Ishmael find when he smashes in the door?
8. What objection does Ishmael have to Queegueg's religion?
9. Why do Bildad and Peleg decide to sign on Queequeg?
10. What is a lay?

Answers

1. Queequeg's idol is named Yojo.
2. Yojo told Queequeg to let Ishmael choose the ship.
3. The *Pequods* are an extinct tribe of Indians.
4. The *Pequod's* winches and tiller are made of whale bone.
5. Two Quakers, Bildad and Peleg, are the owners.
6. Tistig predicted that Ahab would be like the vile biblical King Ahab.
7. Ishmael finds Queequeg squatting in the middle of the floor with Yojo on his head.
8. Ishmael objects to harmful, radical religious practices.
9. Queequeg proves his skill with the harpoon by hitting a small drop of tar on the water.
10. The lay is the share of the profit a seaman earns.

Suggested Essay Topics

1. Trace the development of the religious theme in this section.

Consider Queequeg's practices and beliefs, Ishmael's ambiguous feelings, and the behavior of the two Quakers.

2. Explain how Melville piques our curiosity about Ahab. Include not only Peleg's description of him, but also his experience with Ahab.

Chapters XIX – XXV

New Characters:

Elijah: *a strange, ragged old man; a prophet of doom*

Aunt Charity: *Bildad's sister*

Summary

As Queequeg and Ishmael approach the *Pequod*, which is being made ready for its long voyage, they are accosted by Elijah, who makes many vague and unsettling innuendos about the ship and its captain, whom he calls Old Thunder.

The morning the ship is to set sail, Ishmael sees some "shadows," which he takes to be men, boarding the boat. Elijah approaches him once again and tells him to see if he can find those sailors when he goes aboard. Although Ahab had come on the ship the night before sailing, he has remained in his cabin.

The ship sets sail on Christmas morning, piloted out of port by Bildad and Peleg. When it is time for them to leave the ship, they are reluctant to go. That night, Ishmael is surprised to see Bulkington at the helm.

Ishmael defends whaling as a noble occupation. Whalers are no more butchers than are soldiers who earn praise for their slaughtering. Whale oil lights the lamps of the world and is used to anoint the heads of kings and queens at their coronations. For Ishmael, whaling was his Harvard and Yale.

Analysis

In the Bible, the first book of Kings, the prophet Elijah is an enemy of the wicked King Ahab. The Elijah who stops Ishmael is

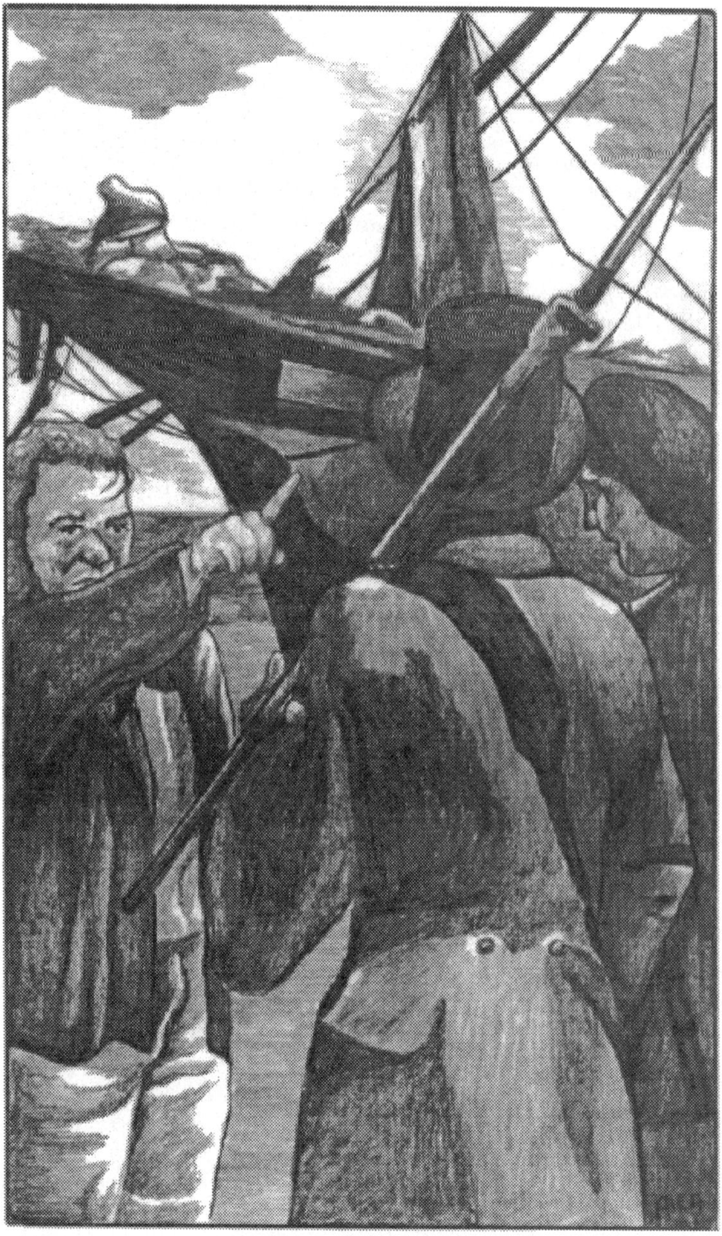

also a prophet. He suggests that Queequeg and Ishmael may have signed over their souls when they signed onto the *Pequod*. He intimates that Ahab lost his leg "according to the prophecy." He also raises the issue of fate when he says, "What's to be, will be ...it's all fixed and arranged a'ready."

Ishmael remarks that he suspects something is amiss, but suppresses his suspicions. "I said nothing, and tried to think nothing." His dismay increases when he sees shadows going onto the boat. These "shadows" will remain a mystery until later in the book.

The *Pequod* sails on Christmas day, and Bildad is singing a hymn "full of hope and fruition" as the boat pulls out of port. Regardless, because of the earlier foreshadowing and the words of Elijah, the reader has a sense of foreboding.

Bulkington, although we see him only briefly, is a significant character. "Land seemed scorching to his feet." In the land/sea duality, the land represents safe, traditional knowledge and belief. On a thematic level, Bulkington is the "deep earnest thinker"; "in landlessness alone resides the truth, shoreless, indefinite as God."

Study Questions

1. Describe Elijah and explain the significance of his name.
2. What nickname does he have for Ahab?
3. What vague references does he make to events in Ahab's past?
4. What effect did Elijah have on Ishmael?
5. Why is Aunt Charity aptly named?
6. Is Ishmael able to find the shadowy figures he saw board the boat?
7. In Queequeg's land, with what do the wealthier people "furnish" their houses?
8. What is the *Pequod*'s day of departure?
9. What are the sailors singing about while Bildad sings his "dismal stave of psalmody?"
10. Who piloted the ship out of the harbor?

Answers

1. Elijah is a ragged, pockmarked old sailor, named after a biblical prophet and enemy of King Ahab.
2. Old Thunder is his nickname for Ahab.
3. He refers to a three-day period when Ahab "lay like dead" and to a deadly scrimmage with a Spaniard.
4. Ishmael felt apprehensive.
5. She worked tirelessly to provide comfort for those going on the voyage.
6. No, and he tried to keep the thought out of his mind.
7. They furnish their houses with fattened, lower class folk to use as settees.
8. Christmas is the *Pequod*'s day of departure.
9. The sailors sing about "the girls in Booble alley."
10. Peleg and Bildad are the pilots.

Suggested Essay Topics

1. Compare the symbolic meaning of the land and the sea, respectively. What is it about the sea that suggests the freedom of thought? What is it about the land that suggests its symbolic meaning? How does Bulkington feel about the sea? Use direct quotations to support your ideas.
2. Discuss how various characters and circumstances provide foreshadowing in this section.

Chapters XXVI – XXXI

New Characters:

Starbuck: *chief mate*

Stubb: *second mate*

Flask: *third mate, called King-Post*

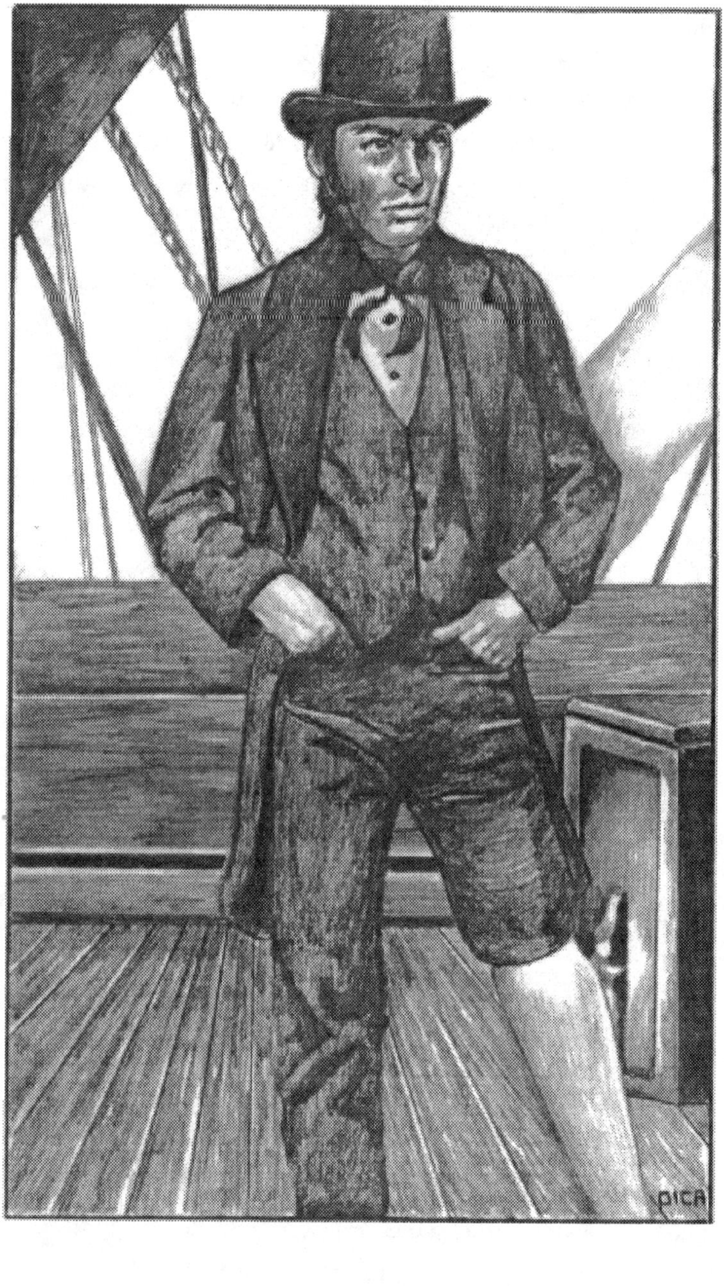

Tashtego: *Stubb's Indian harpooner*
Daggoo: *Flask's African harpooner*

Summary

The first two chapters of this section, both entitled "Knights and Squires," describe the officers of the *Pequod*. "Three better, more likely sea-officers and men, each in his own different way, could not readily be found, and they were every one of them Americans."

Starbuck, a Quaker, is a lean, "steadfast man." He had lost both a father and a brother to whaling and has a family at home. Consequently, he is a cautious whaleman who "will have no man in (his) boat who is not afraid of a whale."

"Happy-go-lucky" Stubb, on the other hand, is "easy and careless" about whaling. His pipe is a permanent feature of his face. It is Stubb who confronts Ahab about his pacing the deck, keeping the crew awake at night with the thumping of his ivory leg. Ahab gets angry and calls him a dog. Stubb at first takes offense, but later, after a dream about Ahab kicking him, decides that an insult from a man like Ahab is, in fact, an honor.

Flask, the third mate, is a "stout, ruddy" fellow called King-Post. Bent on destroying whales, he is fearless as he feels that he has been personally affronted by the creatures.

Ahab at last appears on deck where, eventually, he will stay most of the time. Ishmael is filled with apprehension at his first sight of him. Ahab is branded with a scar that runs down his face into his shirt. He puts the tip of his ivory leg into auger holes, which have been drilled into the deck. Sometimes he sits upon an ivory stool to smoke, but when smoking "no longer soothes," he throws his pipe into the sea.

Analysis

That *Moby-Dick* is a tragedy of epic proportions is made clear to us in this section. Melville uses the classic device of apostrophe to address absent beings or abstract concepts. In an elevated style, he speaks to the "just Spirit of Equality, which hast spread one royal mantle of humanity over all." This apostrophe is not unlike Homer's or Milton's asking the Muses for divine inspiration. Melville explains that he will imbue common men with heroic, "high qualities" and "tragic graces." He asks the Spirit of Equality to intercede for him against critics who object.

The *Pequod* is a microcosm manned by sailors of all races. Melville remarks that most of them are islanders, "isolatoes," living on their own separate continents, but united on this ship—symbolically, the world.

Each mate represents a different approach to whaling and, on a thematic level, to nature and life itself. Starbuck respects the whale as strong and dangerous. He also values life and means to preserve his own. For him, whaling is a way to make a living. Stubb seems to have accepted things as they are and goes about his business cheerfully. Flask sees whales as enemies. He has no reverence for "the many marvels of their majestic bulk and mystic ways."

Study Questions

1. Although Starbuck is as brave as any man, what does he fear?
2. In Melville's tribute to man at the end of Chapter XXVI, what is the source of the common man's "august dignity?"
3. Who are the three mates' harpooners, respectively?
4. How is Tashtego both like and unlike his ancestors?
5. To what animal is Daggoo compared and why is that simile appropriate?
6. What is an "isolato"?
7. "Ahab stood before them with a crucifixion in his face." Explain the meaning of this description.
8. In what way is Ahab like a bare, old oak that sends out a few green sprouts?
9. Describe the Merman of Stubb's dream.
10. In what way is this dream prophetic?

Answers

1. Starbuck cannot stand up to "an enraged and mighty man,"

a hint that he will not be able to stand up to Ahab.
2. "Divine equality" that radiates from God is the source of the common man's dignity.
3. Queequeg is Starbuck's harponer; Stubb's is Tashtego; and Flask's is Daggoo.
4. Tashtego is a "proud warrior hunter," but he hunts whales not moose.
5. The six foot five Daggoo is appropriately compared to a giraffe, another creature of Africa.
6. An "Isolato" is both literally and figuratively an islander, living separate from the mainland.
7. This description emphasizes Ahab's suffering and misery. It may also foreshadow his doom.
8. As the weather grew nicer, Ahab came close to smiling.
9. The Merman is humpbacked and his rump is stuck full of marlin spikes.
10. Moby Dick is humpbacked, and stuck with harpoons. Also, the Merman instructs Stubb not to kick back at Ahab; so Stubb, like Starbuck, will not stand up to him.

Suggested Essay Topics
1. Compare the captain and officers of the *Pequod*: Ahab, Starbuck, Stubb, and Flask. Include physical descriptions, but concentrate on character.
2. What devices of style does Melville use to elevate his tale to tragedy? What is his purpose in doing this? Why does Melville wish to make the common man as noble as a Greek hero?

Chapters XXXII – XXXV

New Character:

Dough-Boy: *the cabin steward*

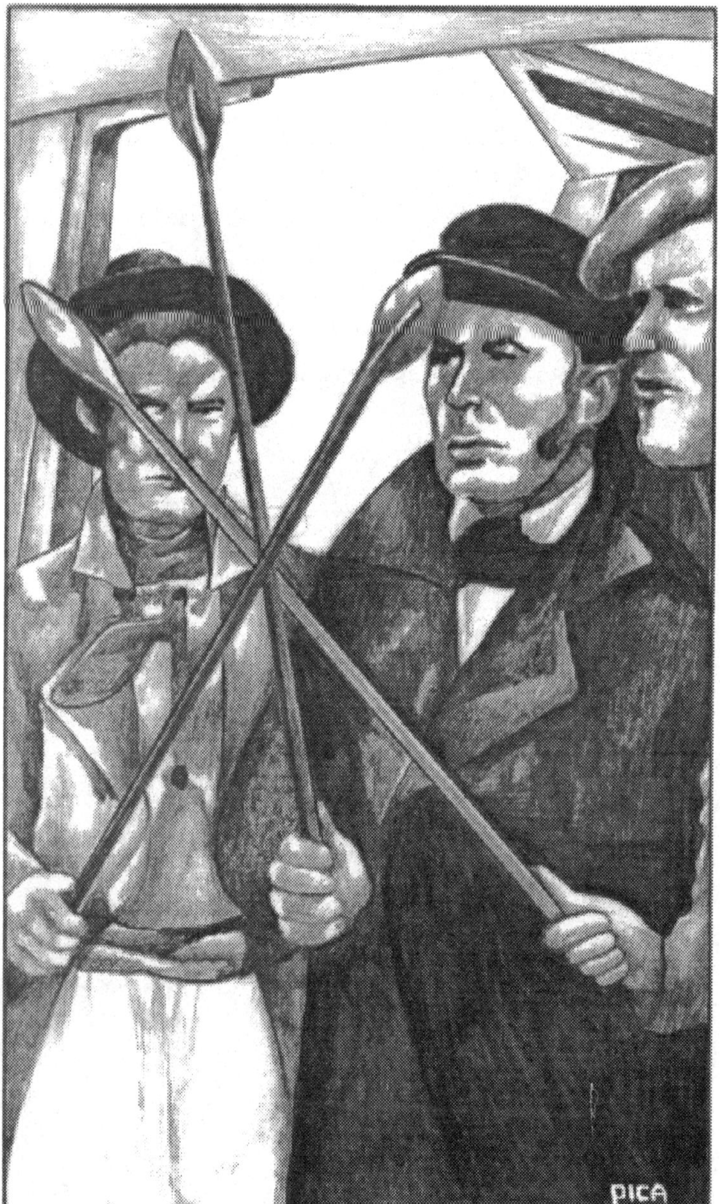
PICA

Chapters XXXII-XXXV

Summary

Ishmael believes that to understand the references to whales that will follow in his narrative, it is first necessary to have some knowledge of the general classifications of whales. He defines the whale as "a spouting fish with a horizontal tail." He then classifies whales according to size into three "books," each with its "chapters." The first book is made of the largest whales, such as the sperm and right whales. The second consists of middle-sized whales, such as the narwhale and killer whale. The last contains porpoises.

Ishmael then explains the hierarchy of the whale ship. The chief harpooner is known as the specksynder. Because ultimately the success of a voyage depends on the harpooners, they are given quarters aft with the captain and mates. General seamen live forward of the mast.

The mates take their meals with the captain in his cabin. With Ahab, this is a silent, solemn affair. After they have left, the harpooners have their dinners. They are so boisterous and lively that they frighten the steward.

Of all the ship's duties, standing the masthead can be most pleasant. On balmy days, Ishmael, standing watch high up on the mast, performs his duty poorly, for he gets lost in the reverie of his thoughts. Unfortunately, whalers that fish in the South Seas are not equipped with crow's nests, and on cold, stormy days, masthead watch is most unpleasant.

Analysis

Like the "Etymology and Extracts" sections that precede the first chapter, the cetology chapter suggests that what we know is open to interpretation, that meaning can be, and often is, ambiguous. Knowledge is also incomplete, as is rightly so according to Ishmael, for the greatest works are those that are left to posterity to finish. Ishmael calls his own work, "but a draught—nay, but the draught of a draught." The cetology chapter demonstrates Ishmael's passion to understand.

The classification of whales and of those who hunt them presents an interesting comparison. Unlike whales, humans depend upon social form, such as who eats in the cabin, to make distinctions among themselves. "For be a man's intellectual superiority what it will, it can never assume...supremacy over other men, without the aid of some sort of external arts...."

Ahab is characterized as alienated. "Though nominally included in the census of Christendom, he was still alien to it." Like a hibernating bear, "Ahab's soul, shut up in the caved trunk of his body, there fed upon the sullen paws of its gloom."

The theme of the spiritual unity of living things is reiterated when Ishmael describes standing duty on the masthead. Young men like Ishmael gaze down at the ocean below and see their identities in the "mystic ocean, the visible image of that deep, blue, bottomless soul, pervading mankind and nature."

Study Questions

1. What is cetology?
2. What whales are in the first category of large whales?
3. What did the term "specksynder" mean originally and what has it come to mean?
4. In what ways does Ahab observe the traditions of his rank?
5. What is the atmosphere of the captain and his mates' dinner?
6. Why does Flask frequently go hungry?
7. What is the atmosphere of the harpooners' dinner?
8. How many masts are kept manned?
9. Upon what do the watches on the mastheads stand?
10. Why does Ishmael keep such a "sorry guard" when he stands the masthead watch?

Answers

1. Cetology is the study of whales.
2. Sperm whales and right whales are among the largest.
3. The specksynder originally was the "fat cutter," but has come to mean chief harpooner.

4. Ahab dines with his officers and demands obedience.
5. Their dinner is silent and constrained.
6. Flask is the last called to dinner, and because the others finish before him, etiquette demands that he stop eating, too.
7. The harpooners fill their bellies, make a lot of commotion, and tease Dough-Boy mercilessly.
8. Three masts are manned.
9. The watches stand on "thin sticks" called gallant cross-trees.
10. Ishmael gets lost in thought and fails to keep a good lookout for whales and squalls.

Suggested Essay Topics

1. Explain the hierarchy of authority on the whaler. What are the "social forms" and customs which support that hierarchy? Give specific examples and describe the customs as they are observed on the *Pequod*.
2. What does the cetology chapter contribute to the theme of man's understanding of his universe? Where is a seaman apt to gain such knowledge? How?

Chapters XXXVI – XL

New Character:

Pip: *the cabin boy*

Summary

Ahab summons all hands to the quarter-deck. He hammers a gold coin to the mast and promises it to the first man who sees the white whale "with a wrinkled brow and a crooked jaw." Ahab admits that it is Moby Dick, the whale that "dismasted" him. He also admits that killing Moby Dick is the purpose of the voyage. He rallies all the men behind him; only Starbuck dissents.

Ahab gathers the crew around him, his hand upon the crossed

lances of his mates. They all drink from a pewter goblet. The harpooners drink from the detached iron spears of their harpoons.

Ahab, alone in his cabin, cannot enjoy the beauty of the sunset. He is "damned in the midst of paradise." He defies the gods that have "knocked (him) down." Starbuck thinks about the power Ahab has over him. He is tied to him and, though rebelling, must obey. Stubb tells himself that all is predestined and the only thing to do is laugh about it.

The sailors drink, dance, sing, and fight until a squall comes up and they must reef the masts. Pip, the frightened cabin boy, prays to the "big white God" to have mercy on a little black boy.

Analysis

Stubb, observing Ahab, tells Flask, " ...the chick that's in him pecks the shell. `Twill soon be out." That "chick" is Ahab's monomaniacal desire for revenge on Moby Dick.

When Starbuck tells Ahab it is blasphemous to exact vengeance from a dumb brute that "simply smote thee from blindest instinct," Ahab replies that to him the whale represents evil. The whale is a mask, a wall, behind which is the reality: "inscrutable malice." Ahab believes his "high perception" has damned him and driven him to madness. "What I've dared, I've willed; and what I've willed, I'll do. They think me mad...but I'm demoniac, I am madness maddened."

Melville takes great liberties with the narrative form in this section. In "Sunset," the point of view changes from Ishmael's first person point of view to Ahab's internal monologue. Similarly, internal monologues are used for Starbuck and Stubb. "Midnight, Forecastle" is a play, stage directions and all.

Color imagery develops importance in this section. The white whale represents evil to Ahab. The white God is salvation to Pip. Daggoo says he is "quarried" out of blackness and fights with a white Spaniard over the color issue. Ahab's white scar is compared to the lightning bolt in the sky.

Study Questions

1. What does Ahab nail to the mast?
2. Who will win the Spanish coin?

Chapters XXXVI-XL

3. What distinguishing characteristics does Moby Dick have?
4. Who objects to Ahab's purpose?
5. What is Ahab's emotional state as he talks of the whale's taking off his leg?
6. What sound comes from the hold?
7. On what does Ahab place his hand as the crew swears an oath?
8. What is the oath the crew swears?
9. What is Stubb's reaction to all that has happened?
10. What are some of the nationalities represented by the sailors?

Answers

1. Ahab nails a Spanish doubloon to the mast.
2. The man who first sights Moby Dick will win the coin.
3. Moby Dick has a white head, a wrinkled brow, a crooked jaw, and a spout like a shock of wheat.
4. Starbuck objects to Ahab's purpose.
5. He becomes intensely emotional and angry, making a sound like an animal sob.
6. A low laugh comes from the hold.
7. Ahab places his hand on the three crossed harpoons.
8. The crew's oath is "Death to Moby Dick!"
9. Stubb chooses to laugh at whatever may come.
10. The nationalities include Chinese, French, Spanish, African, Portuguese, and Danish.

Suggested Essay Topics

1. Explain and comment on Starbuck's argument *against* hunting Moby Dick. Explain and comment on Ahab's argument *for* hunting Moby Dick. For what reasons does Starbuck acquiesce?

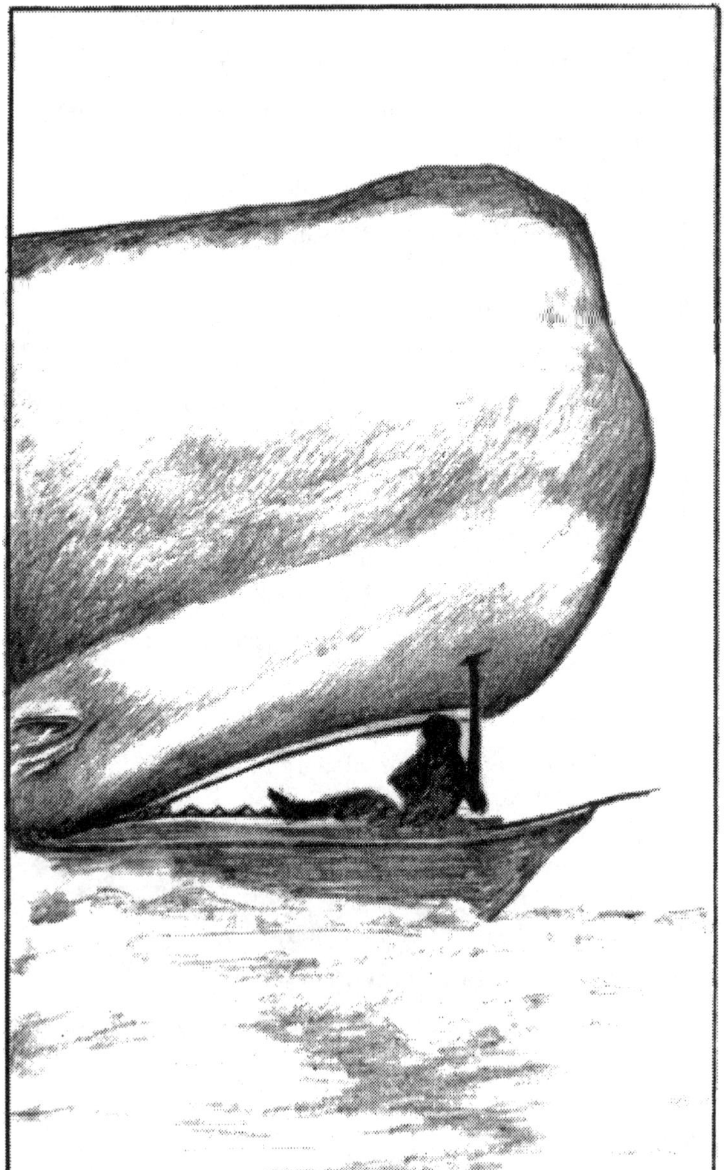

2. Describe the tactics Ahab uses to bind the men to him. Does it work? Describe the crew's celebration.

Chapters XLI – XLII

Summary

As encounters with Moby Dick become more frequent among whalers, rumors about him grow more fantastic. Some say he is ubiquitous, that he could be in two places at once. Others say that he is immortal. Many ascribe to the creature a kind of malignant intelligence.

Ishmael learns more about Ahab's encounter with Moby Dick. His three boats stove in and his crew swirling in the eddies, Ahab futilely plunged a six-inch blade into the whales's flank. It was then that Moby Dick took his leg in his great, crooked jaw.

Ahab's madness came upon him during the homeward voyage. For months, he lay in his hammock, "his torn body and gashed soul bled into one another" and so made him mad. Later he was able to hide this madness. The Nantucketers believed that his going back out to sea was the best thing for him.

Ishmael speculates on Ahab's and his own feelings for Moby Dick. Ahab "piled upon the whale's white hump the sum of all the general rage and hate felt by his whole race from Adam down." For Ahab, Moby Dick embodies the very essence of evil. Ishmael's feelings for the whale have more to do with its color. Although whiteness may signify beauty and innocence, it is also the color of the horse upon which Death rides and the color of a corpse's skin. More frightening to Ishmael is that whiteness is an absence. It is blankness.

Analysis

"Moby Dick" and "The Whiteness of the Whale" are more attempts by Ishmael to comprehend. In these chapters, he analyzes and reasons, but admits that "to explain, would be to dive deeper than Ishmael can go." Furthermore, he hints at an ambiguity of feeling for Moby Dick; for at the beginning of his chapter on whiteness, he uses the qualifying phrase, "what *at times* he was to me."

Regardless, Ishmael is bound to Ahab and seems fated to help him in his revenge. "Here, then, was this grey-headed, ungodly old man, chasing a whale round the world, at the head of a crew made up of mongrel renegades, and castaways, and cannibals...specially picked by some infernal fatality...." This description emphasizes the contrast between the majestic whale and the rag-tag band hunting him. It also suggests the futility of striking out against Moby Dick and what he symbolizes.

Ishmael's voyage, figuratively, is a quest to know, to understand. The "nameless horror" embodied in the whale's whiteness is, at best, that there is no absolute meaning. Ishmael explains how whiteness can be interpreted as both good and evil. "...whiteness is...the visible absence of color, and at the same time the concrete of all colors." At worst, the "nameless horror" is that the universe has no meaning at all. "Nature...paints like the harlot, whose allurements cover nothing but the charnel house within...."

Study Questions

1. What were some of the wild rumors about Moby Dick?
2. Why were Moby Dick's "retreats" feared more than anything?
3. With what did Ahab attack Moby Dick?
4. How is Moby Dick's deformed jaw shaped?
5. Figuratively, what did Ahab pile upon the whale's white hump?
6. When was Ahab seized with his monomania?
7. Where had Ishmael first seen an albatross?
8. What impression did it make on him at the time?
9. What white creature is famous in American western legend?
10. What was it about the whale that instilled horror in Ishmael?

Answers

1. Rumors spread that Moby Dick was ubiquitous and immortal.

2. He was known to turn around suddenly and attack.
3. Ahab attacked Moby Dick with only a small knife.
4. Moby Dick's jaw is sickle-shaped.
5. He piled on the general rage and hate that all men have felt toward intangible evil.
6. Ahab was seized with his monomania as he lay suffering during the long voyage home.
7. Ishmael found an albatross dashed upon the deck when he sailed the Antarctic.
8. Ishmael was struck with wonder and bowed before the albatross. He considered it mystical.
9. The White Steed of the Prairies is famous in American western legend.
10. The whiteness of the whale instilled horror in Ishmael.

Suggested Essay Topics

1. Discuss the ambiguities associated with the meanings of whiteness. Choose several examples from Ishmael's explanation to illustrate both the positive and negative interpretations. Why is Ishmael so appalled by the whiteness of Moby Dick?

2. Describe the legends that surround Moby Dick. What is actually known about him? What does he look like? Explain Ahab's encounter with him. Describe Ahab's suffering. What has the whale come to symbolize to him?

Chapters XLIII – XLVII

New Characters:

Archy and Cabaco: *sailors aboard the* Pequod

Summary

Archy hears coughs from under the hatches where no one should be. Cabaco tells him it must be something he ate. Every night in his cabin, Ahab studies nautical charts trying to map out the most likely path to bring him to Moby Dick. For several years the whale has been sighted at the time and place known as Season-on-the-Line. The Season will not occur for another year, but in the meantime, Ahab plots the migratory patterns of sperm whales.

Ishmael offers proof for all he has said about whales. Whales do have recognizable traits and are given names such as Rinaldo Rinaldini, Timor Tom, Don Miguel, and others. Sperm whales have destroyed entire ships such as the *Essex* out of Nantucket.

By using the *Pequod* for his own purposes, Ahab has left himself open to the charge of usurpation. The crew would be legally justified in a mutiny. He must hunt for other whales in order to appease the crew, particularly Starbuck.

As Queequeg and Ishmael are working together weaving a mat, Tashtego cries out, "There she blows!" The men, lowering their boats, see "five dusky phantoms" preparing to join Ahab in the hunt.

Analysis

Archy's suspicions are proven sound when the five phantoms are seen with Ahab. These are the shadows Ishmael saw boarding the ship in Nantucket.

Melville further explores the theme of vengeance. "What trances of torments does that man endure who is consumed with one unachieved revengeful desire. He sleeps with clenched hands; and wakes with his own bloody nails in his palms." Ahab wakens from his dreams with wild cries and runs from his stateroom. It is

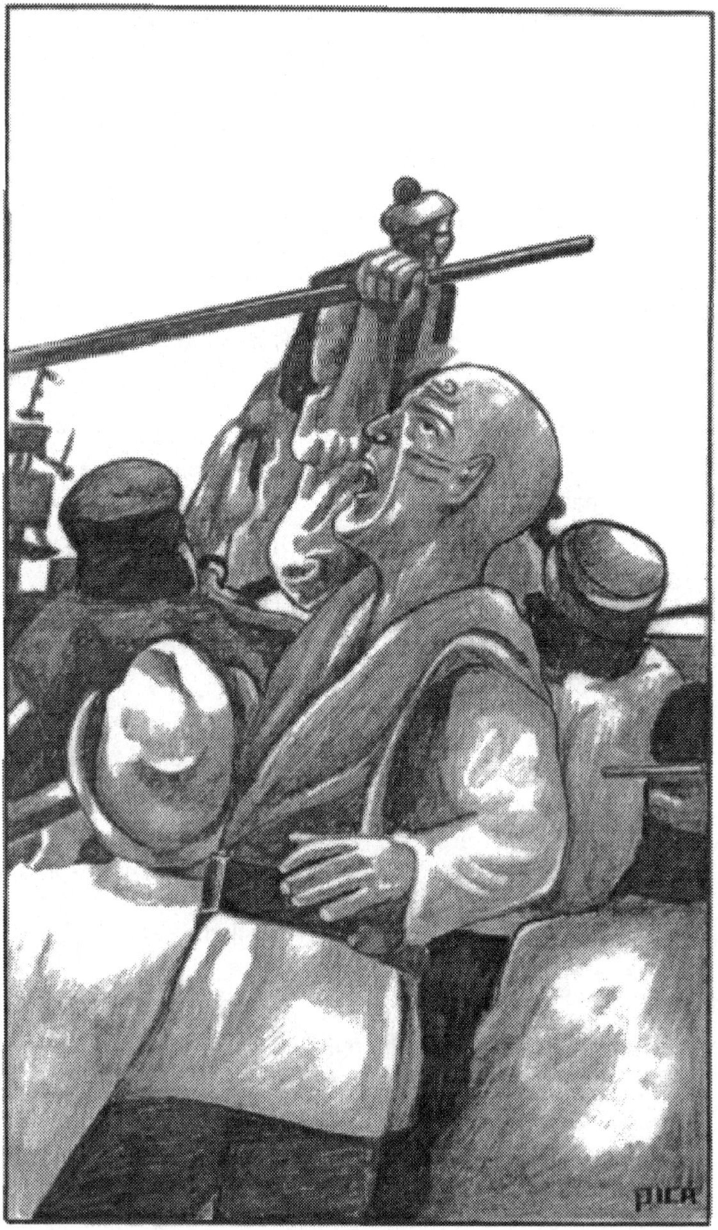

his soul that cries out and runs in terror of the crazy Ahab. The concept of dualistic man is here emphasized.

In a classical allusion, Ahab is compared to Prometheus, the Greek god who gave fire to man. He is punished by being bound on a mountain where an eagle eats out his liver. In Ahab's case, a "vulture," his vengeance, eats out his heart.

Ishmael believes the mat that he and Queequeg weave is symbolic of necessity, free will, and chance. He calls their weaving "the Loom of Time." Weaving and knitting are frequently symbols of fate.

Study Questions

1. Who, other than Archy, suspects stowaways are on board?
2. What problem has the departure date of the *Pequod* posed for Ahab?
3. What often forced Ahab from his hammock at night?
4. Who are Don Miguel and New Zealand Jack?
5. What proof does Ishmael offer that the public is unaware of the dangers of whaling?
6. What happened to the *Essex*?
7. How does Ishmael know the story of the *Essex*?
8. Why must Ahab hunt other whales even though killing Moby Dick is his real purpose?
9. Who weaves the mat?
10. Where have the five phantoms been seen before?

Answers

1. Archy says he heard Stubb tell Flask something about it.
2. Ahab has to wait another year before it will again be the Season-on-the-Line.
3. Ahab was plagued by horrible dreams.
4. They are two of the many famous whales who have earned names.

5. Not one in fifty of the fatalities is reported because communication is so slow.
6. A big sperm whale rammed the *Essex* and sank her.
7. Ishmael knew the chief mate and the son of her captain.
8. Ahab could be charged with usurpation of the ship and his crew could legally take away his command.
9. Ishmael and Queequeg weave the mat.
10. Ishmael saw the phantoms board the *Pequod* in Nantucket.

Suggested Essay Topics

1. Discuss the symbolic meaning of the mat-making. First describe how Ishmael and Queequeg make the mat. Then explain what each component of the process symbolizes. Finally, tell why Ishmael's interpretation is appropriate for the steps involved.
2. Ishmael frequently strays from his narrative to interject facts about whales and whaling, as he does in "The Affidavit." What is an affidavit and why is it an appropriate title for this chapter? What is the content, tone, and purpose of the chapter?

Chapters XLVIII – LI

New Character:

Fedallah: *Ahab's mysterious harpooner*

Summary

Ahab's boat is lowered by Fedallah and his crew. Fedallah is tall and dark and has one tooth protruding from his lips. His braided white hair is wrapped around his head like a turban. Ahab takes his place at the helm of his whale boat. All the other boats are lowered as well.

Just as Queequeg throws his harpoon at a whale, the boat is swamped. Ishmael, Starbuck, and the others are thrown from the

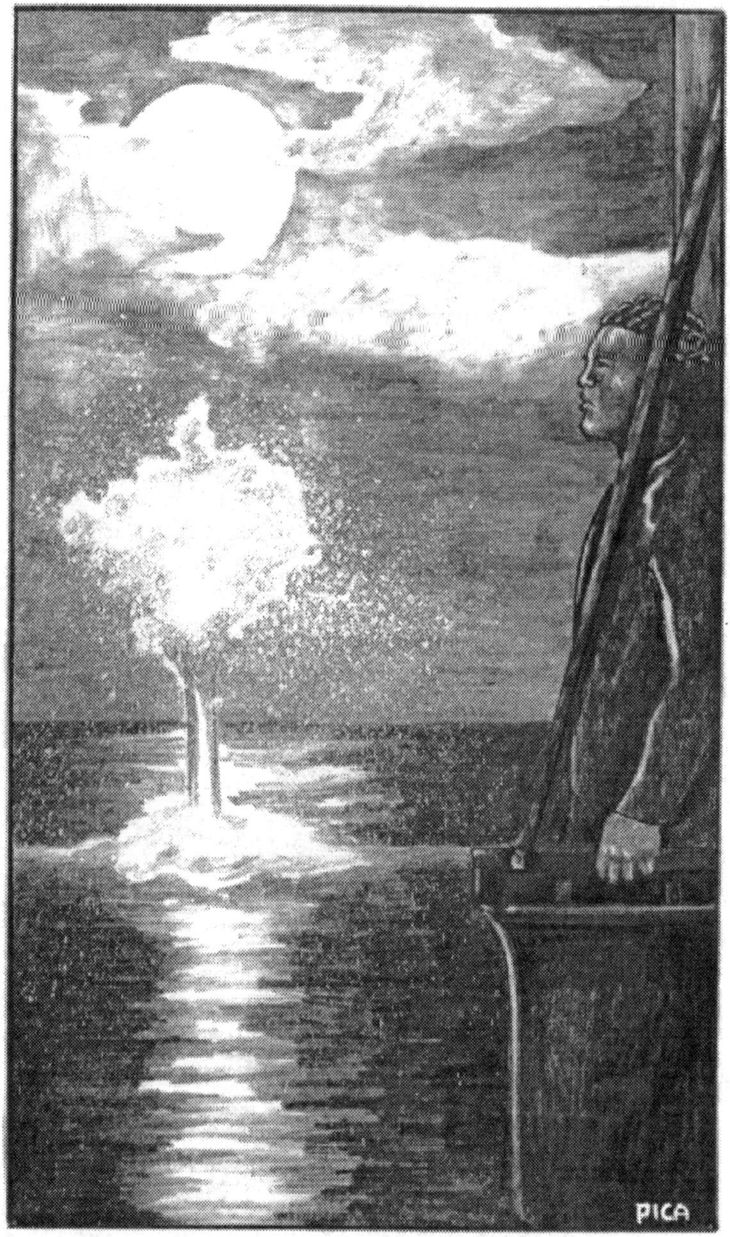
PICA

boat, but manage to pull themselves back in. They are separated from the others and lost all night in the storm and fog. At dawn, the *Pequod* finds them. After this incident, Ishmael makes out a will.

Fedallah spots a silvery spout. The *Pequod* is never able to catch up with it although it appears every night at midnight. As the ship nears the Cape of Good Hope, the weather becomes cold; the ocean, treacherous.

Analysis

Fedallah is associated with evil. When Ahab questions him, Fedallah "hisses" a reply. He is dark and dressed in "funereal" black. Ishmael imagines him the offspring of the devil who "consorted with the daughters of men." Fedallah's crew are yellow-complexioned Manillans, believed to be agents of the devil by some sailors.

Fedallah and his crew are described as "dusky phantoms fresh formed out of air." On a symbolic level, they are spiritual for they represent Ahab's dark alter ego emerging as he comes closer to the object of his vengeance. Similarly, the spirit-spout, believed to be that of Moby Dick, represents the vengeance luring Ahab to destruction.

At the same time, the spirit-spout is spotted, flocks of sea-ravens perch upon the stays as if the *Pequod* is uninhabited, "a thing appointed to desolation." The heaving black sea is metaphorically compared to a conscience "in anguish" for the "suffering it had bred." The atmosphere of "The Spirit-Spout" chapter is grim and foreboding.

Ishmael's writing his will seems an acquiescence to his fate. His acceptance of his mortality takes a weight from his heart. "Here goes for a cool, collected dive at death and destruction," he tells himself jokingly, expressing his new "desperado philosophy."

Study Questions

1. Of what is Fedallah's turban made?
2. Why was Ahab's boat able to outrun the others?
3. What did Flask do in order to gain a better vantage from

which to spot the whales who had sounded below the water?

4. Whose boat was separated from the *Pequod* for the entire night?
5. Of the mates, which one has the reputation of being most prudent?
6. What does Ishmael do after having his near death experience?
7. Why would Bildad and Peleg never have granted Ahab a whale boat of his own?
8. Why were Fedallah and his crew able to "find a place among the crew"?
9. What did Fedallah spot on his midnight watch?
10. What did Starbuck see when he looked in on Ahab?

Answers

1. Fedallah's braided white hair coils around his head like a turban.
2. His phantom crew rowed like "five trip-hammers."
3. Flask stood on Daggoo's shoulders.
4. Starbuck's boat was lost in the fog.
5. Starbuck has the reputation of being exceedingly cautious.
6. Ishmael makes out his will.
7. Captains usually didn't get directly involved in the hunts, and Captain Ahab's disability could put both himself and his men in unnecessary danger.
8. Fedallah and his crew had shown themselves to be able crewmen, and whalers are used to seeing all manner of men from the "nooks and ash-holes of the world."
9. Fedallah spotted the spirit spout.
10. Starbuck saw Ahab sleeping straight up in his chair, sleet dripping from him.

Suggested Essay Topics

1. Compare and contrast the ways in which the three mates react to the sight of Fedallah and his crew. Also, compare the ways in which they command their respective boats. Give specific details of what they say and do. How does this section further develop the characterization of these men?

2. Describe the atmosphere of "The Spirit-Spout," choosing central images from the chapter and explaining how they create this atmosphere. Consider sound as well as visual imagery.

Chapters LII – LIV

New Characters:

Radney: *mate on the* Town-Ho

Steelkilt: *sailor on the* Town-Ho

Dons Pedro and Sebastian: *young men to whom Ishmael told the* Town-Ho's *story*

The *Albatross*: *ship with which the* Pequod *has an unsuccessful gam*

The *Town-Ho*: *ship manned by Polynesians*

Summary

Southwest of the Cape of Good Hope, the *Pequod* meets the *Albatross*, a ship heading home after a four-year voyage. Ahab hails the ship asking if they have seen the White Whale. As the other captain is about to reply, he drops the horn through which he was about to speak into the water. His reply is lost in the wind.

This meeting, peculiar to whaleships, is known as a gam. Frequently, the boats' crews exchange visits, mail, papers, and whaling news.

The *Pequod* then has a short gam with the *Town-Ho* from which much is learned about the White Whale. Ishmael hears a secret part of the story, from Tashtego.

Two years earlier, the *Town-Ho* was sailing the Pacific when

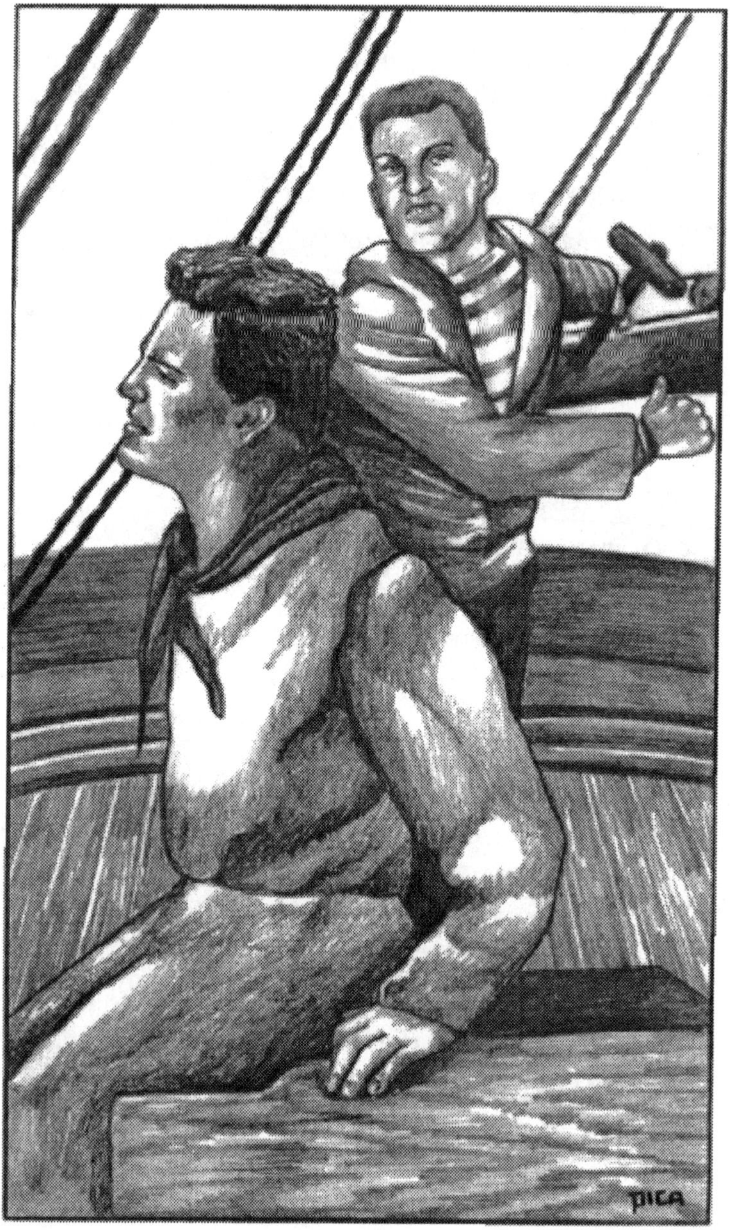
PICA

Chapters LII-LIV

the ship sprang a leak. Among the sailors laboring at the pumps was a "tall, noble animal" named Steelkilt. Just as Steelkilt sat down to rest, the ugly first mate, Radney, ordered him to shovel up some pig droppings from the deck. Steelkilt refused. Radney came at Steelkilt with a hammer, and Steelkilt punched him in the mouth.

Steelkilt and some of his allies chose to be locked in the hold, rather than lashed. When they finally came out, the captain lashed the two allies, but didn't dare touch Steelkilt who had whispered some threat. Radney, however, grabbed the rope and lashed Steelkilt himself.

Steelkilt planned Radney's murder, but was saved the effort when the *Town-Ho* came upon Moby Dick. Radney, tossed from his whaleboat, was seized in the jaws of the great whale.

Analysis

The meeting with the *Albatross* reinforces a theme articulated earlier in the book: alienation. Communication between the two ships is thwarted just as it is among the "isolatoes" of the world.

The seamen of the *Pequod* are dismayed by the "ominous incident" at the first mention of Moby Dick. Ahab himself seems saddened when he sees the schools of little fish that had been swimming alongside the *Pequod* for days dart away toward the *Albatross*. Ahab becomes a pariah to nature as he seeks his vengeance on the White Whale.

Although part of the story as a whole, the *Town-Ho* narrative, is somewhat removed from it by a double framing device. Ishmael relates the story as he told it to Dons Pedro and Sebastian at an inn in Lima. The dialogue of these characters is interjected throughout the story and at the end, Ishmael swears on a Bible that what he has told them is the truth.

To Ishmael, the *Town-Ho*'s encounter with Moby Dick seemed predestined. "A strange fatality pervades the whole career of these events, as if verily mapped out before the world itself was charted." In this story, Moby Dick saves Steelkilt from the "damning thing he would have done." That Moby Dick can be heaven's minion to Steelkilt and the essence of evil to Ahab is another demonstration of the ambiguity in human perception.

Study Questions

1. Why does the *Albatross* have a spectral appearance?
2. What was the "ominous incident" that occurred when the *Pequod* met the *Albatross*?
3. Why was Ahab bothered by the fish swimming away from his ship to follow the *Albatross*?
4. What is a gam?
5. When a captain is being rowed to another boat for a gamming, why is his position precarious?
6. What is the frame in which the *Town-Ho*'s story is told?
7. When did the incident involving Radney and Steelkilt occur?
8. What was the source of Radney's hatred of Steelkilt?
9. What role did Moby Dick play in their conflict?
10. Why was the *Town-Ho* manned by Polynesians when it gammed with the *Pequod*?

Answers

1. The ship has been at sea for four years.
2. The captain of the *Albatross* dropped his speaking horn into the ocean when Ahab asked about Moby Dick.
3. Ahab felt as if the fish were turning from him personally.
4. A gam is a meeting of two whale ships whose crews visit and exchange letters, papers, and whaling news.
5. The captain must stand and keep his balance while the sea pitches the boat and the oars hit him in the knees and back.
6. Ishmael tells the story in an inn in Lima.
7. The incident took place two years earlier.
8. Although Radney was in command, Steelkilt was the superior man.
9. Moby Dick killed Radney before Steelkilt had a chance.
10. The crew deserted the *Town-Ho* when it reached an island

port, and the captain had to man it with Polynesians.

Suggested Essay Topics
1. Briefly summarize the significant events of the *Town-Ho* story and explain its thematic importance. What role does Moby Dick play in the story? In what way is he an avenging angel?
2. Describe the *Albatross*. How do its appearance and the events that occur during the thwarted gam create an ominous atmosphere? How does Ahab feel after the gam? Why?

Chapters LV – LX

Summary

Few pictures of whales are accurate because the true majesty of the whale can be seen only in unfathomable waters. However, there are many pictures of whales. A crippled beggar in London holds a painted board depicting the scene in which he lost his leg. Sailors carve and etch whale bone and whale teeth, a craft called scrimshanding or scrimshaw. With imagination, whales can be seen in the stars and in undulating mountain ridges.

The *Pequod* cruises through a meadow of brit, the yellow substance eaten by right whales. Daggoo raises the cry for the White Whale, but what he has sighted is really a huge, white squid. Starbuck considers it a bad omen.

Typically, the whaling line, the line attached to the harpoon, is run through a series of complicated turns from bow to stern, enclosing the six-man crew in its coils.

Analysis

In this section, the reportorial style of the material devoted to the pictures of whales contrasts with the more poetic style of descriptive passages such as this:

"But one transparent blue morning,...when the long burnished sun-glade on the waters seemed a golden finger laid across them ..., when the slippered waves whispered together...; in this profound hush...a strange spectre was seen."

The "spectre" is the squid. The diction used to describe its appearance creates a mystical atmosphere, as does the use of the biblical word in the line: "Lo! in the same spot where it sank, once more it slowly rose."

The theme of the duality of man is repeated when Ishmael compares the land and sea. "...do you not find a strange analogy to something in yourself?" he asks his readers. The analogy refers to man's savage, untamed nature represented by the sea and to his gentle, peaceful nature represented by an island in that sea. Never venture from that metaphorical island, he says, for there is no return. Ahab is one who has done that, both literally and figuratively.

The unity of man is suggested in the image of the whale line, but the image is not positive. All humans are connected by virtue of the fact that they are all in the same mess, so to speak. "All men live enveloped in whale-lines...but it is only when caught in the swift, sudden turn of death, that mortals realize the silent, subtle , ever-present perils of life."

Study Questions

1. From what have most scientific drawings been done?
2. Where can the most ancient portrait of a whale be found?
3. Who have created the best pictures of whales?
4. What scene is depicted on the beggar's board?
5. What does Ishmael imagine when he gazes at the stars?
6. What is brit?
7. What sound do right whales make when they feed?
8. What is the superstition regarding the white squid?
9. What has caused man to lose his awe of the sea?
10. Why is the whale line a danger to the whalers?

Answers

1. Most have been drawn from dead whales.
2. The oldest portrait is in a cavern-pagoda in India.

3. The French have created the most accurate pictures.
4. The scene in which the beggar lost his leg is depicted.
5. Wearing harpoons for spurs and anchors for bridle-bits, Ishmael imagines that he rides a whale through the skie.
6. Brit is a floating, yellow substance made up of minute marine organisms.
7. They make a sound like the swinging of mower's scythes.
8. Whalemen believed that few whaleships ever beheld the great squid and returned to their ports to tell of it.
9. Man's pride in his science has caused him to lose his awe of the oceans.
10. The whale line encompasses all the men in the boat.

Suggested Essay Topics

1. Explain the analogy Ishmael makes between the land and the sea and mankind. What are the different qualities of the land and the sea, respectively? To what in man do these qualities correspond?
2. Describe the diction used in the chapter devoted to the squid. Mention specific images and figures of speech. How does this style differ from that of the "pictures of whales" chapters? Explain.

Chapters LXI – LXVI

New Character:

Fleece: *a 90-year-old, black cook*

Summary

Drowsing during his watch at the foremast-head, Ishmael, spots a gigantic sperm whale lolling in the tranquil waters of the Indian Ocean. The boats are lowered; Tashtego harpoons the whale; and Stubb kills it with his lance.

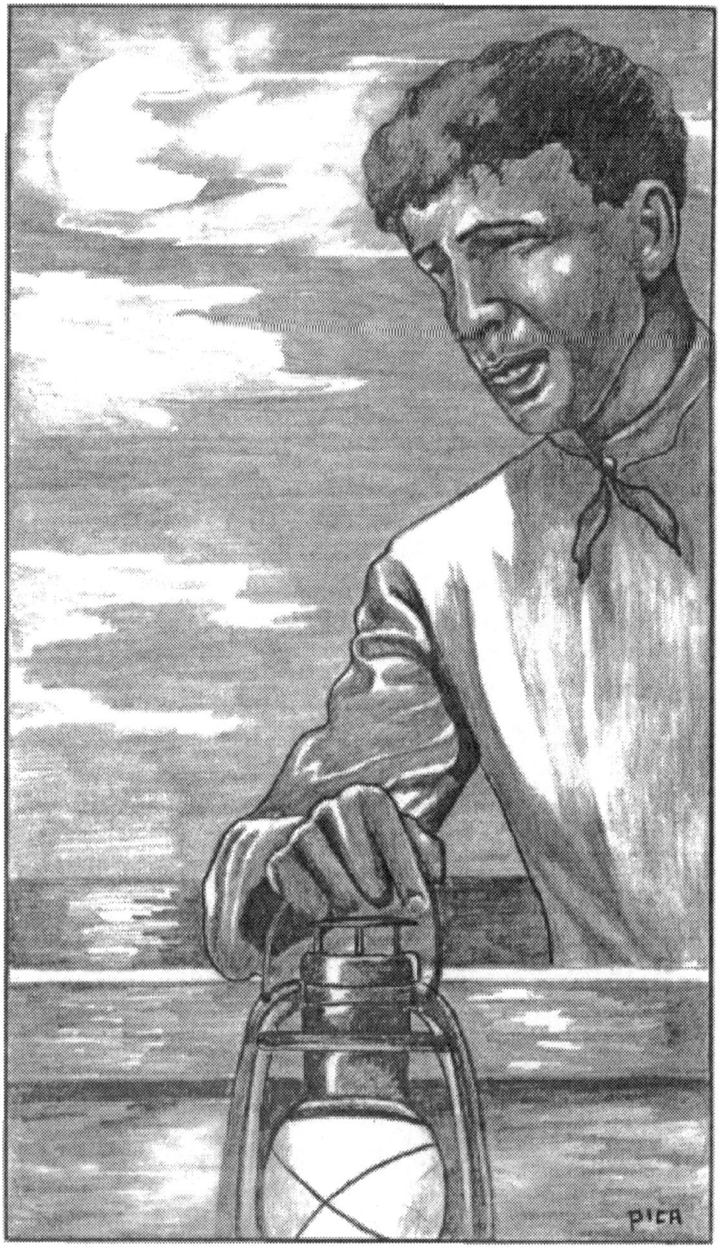
PICA

"It is the harpooneer that makes the voyage." He must cast his harpoon 20 or 30 feet after rowing with all his strength and shouting loudly at the same time. Two harpoons are set in the crotch, but the second is usually thrown overboard where it dangles dangerously from the main harpoon line.

The whale is secured next to the *Pequod*. Stubb tries to enjoy his whale steak dinner, but is disturbed by the noise of the sharks. He tells Fleece to speak to the sharks and quiet them. Futilely, Fleece delivers a sermon and benediction.

During the night, Queequeg and another seaman try to protect the whale carcass by killing sharks with their sharp whaling-spades.

Analysis

A drowsy, tranquil scene opens chapter LXI. Ishmael, on masthead watch, idly sways in the "enchanted air." In his dreamy mood, his soul goes out of his body. He and the other two masthead watches "lifelessly swung from the spars." The imagery creates a sleepy, sultry atmosphere, but, at the same time, suggests the crucifixion scene.

The atmosphere and imagery in the first part of chapter LXI contrast with that of the last part. The tranquil atmosphere becomes a wild chase. Dreamy images become realistic images of the kill as "gush after gush of clotted red gore...shot into the afrighted air."

Several parallels are drawn between the whale and its hunters. The whale is lolling about like the men on the ship; a "jet of white smoke was agonizingly shot from the spiracle of the whale" as puff after puff of smoke came from the mouth of the excited Stubb. When the whale dies, Stubb's pipe goes out.

Man and shark are not so unlike either. During sea battles, the sharks in the water fight over the bodies fallen overboard as the men on deck fight with each other. "...turn the whole affair upside down, it would still be pretty much the same thing."

Fleece's sermon to the sharks, delivered in the old black man's dialect, is wryly humorous. Fleece addresses the sharks as "Belubed fellow critters" and comes to the conclusion that Stubb is more of a shark than a shark. The chapter reiterates the theme of the dual nature of man and the necessity to control the dark side.

Study Questions
1. What does Queequeg say the sighting of the squid means?
2. Where is the *Pequod*?
3. What color is the whale and why is that significant?
4. How far was Stubb's whaleboat towed by the whale?
5. What is the "gold watch" Stubb seeks?
6. What is the primary cause of unsuccessful whaling voyages?
7. How does Ahab feel about this successful hunt?
8. Who is Fleece and what does Stubb demand of him?
9. What moral advice does Fleece give the sharks?
10. What wish does Fleece express that could be considered foreshadowing?

Answers
1. Queequeg says the squid is a sign that a sperm whale will soon be sighted.
2. The *Pequod* is in the Indian Ocean.
3. The whale is black, the opposite of the whale Ahab seeks.
4. "Whole Atlantics and Pacifics seemed passed" describes the distance.
5. The watch is a metaphor for the "innermost life" of the whale.
6. Inefficiency regarding the many tasks of the harpooner and his subsequent exhaustion cause unsuccessful whale hunts.
7. Ahab feels impatience and despair since Moby Dick remains to be killed.
8. Fleece is the old black cook who prepares a whale steak for Stubb and then is told to quiet the sharks.
9. He tells them to share, to help the weaker sharks, to be civilized, to control their shark natures.

10. He wishes "whale eat" Stubb.

Suggested Essay Topics
1. Discuss the techniques Melville uses to equate man to sea creatures. What themes are developed through the comparison?
2. Analyze the imagery at the opening of chapter LXI and compare it to the imagery used to describe the whale chase. What is the effect of this contrast?

Chapters LXVII – LXXI

New Characters:

Captain Mayhew: *captain of the* Jeroboam

Gabriel: *crazed prophet and crewman on the* Jeroboam

Macey: Jeroboam's *chief mate killed by Moby Dick*

The *Jeroboam:* *ship plagued by an epidemic*

Summary
On Sunday, a pulley system is rigged to the mast and a hook is attached to a huge strip of blubber. The strip of blubber is peeled from the whale like a peel from an orange. Starbuck and Stubb stand on staging just above the whale and simultaneously cut a scarf line with their sharp shovels. The whale spins like a log in the water as the spiraled blubber, called the blanket, is hoisted up.

The headless carcass of the whale is set adrift. The head has been hoisted about halfway out of the water against the side of the ship. Ahab speaks to the head telling it to reveal all the secrets it knows.

The *Jeroboam* approaches, but because of an epidemic on his ship, Captain Mayhew speaks to Ahab from his whaleboat. One of his oarsmen is the crazed Gabriel, who tells Ahab to "beware of the blasphemer's end." As Gabriel had predicted, the chief mate of the *Jeroboam* was killed by Moby Dick, whom Gabriel believes to

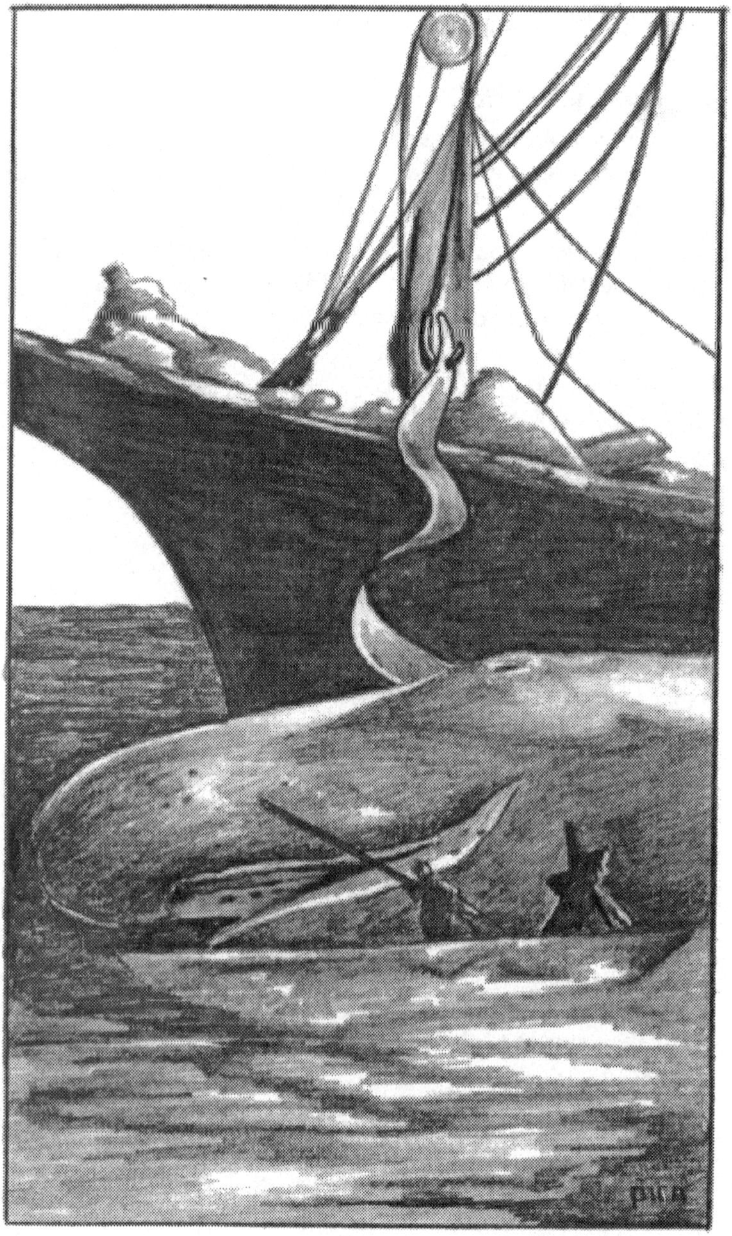

Chapters LXVII-LXXI

be his Shaker god. Ironically, the *Pequod* is carrying a letter for the deceased Macey. When Ahab tries to hand it over, Gabriel grabs it, pierces it with a knife, and throws the knife at Ahab's feet.

Analysis

Once again, the inscrutability of nature is suggested. The whale's skin is crisscrossed with "hieroglyphical" lines, but "the mystic-marked whale remains undecipherable." This passage suggests that Moby Dick will remain undecipherable as well.

That Moby Dick is an ambiguous symbol is further illustrated by Gabriel's belief in him as the Shaker god. The Shakers, a celibate religious sect, maintain that God is a duality, both male and female, the parents of mankind. The two madmen, Ahab and Gabriel, constitute another duality: to one, Moby Dick is the incarnation of God; to the other, the incarnation of evil.

Ahab's speech to the whale's head is also about the inscrutability of nature—in this case represented by the sea. To Ahab, the sea is that "awful water-land" in which the whale has seen all manner of death. The sea is the "murderous hold of this frigate earth ballasted with bones of millions of the drowned..." Ahab asks the head to share the secrets of the sea deaths it has witnessed. "O head!" Ahab apostrophizes, "Thou hast seen enough to split the planets and make an infidel of Abraham."

Study Questions

1. How is blubber removed from the whale?
2. Why is the word "blanket" an appropriate term?
3. Who cuts the scarf line into the blubber?
4. Who attends the whale funeral?
5. What fraction of a whale is made up of its head?
6. To what does Ishmael compare the whale head? Why?
7. Why does Captain Mayhew not board the *Pequod* as is the custom?
8. How do the men aboard the *Jeroboam* feel about Gabriel?
9. Specifically, how was Macey killed?

10. Why would Gabriel think an attack on Moby Dick was blasphemy?

Answers
1. The blubber is peeled off in a spiral. A hook on a pulley draws the huge strip up the mast.
2. The blanket, or blubber, keeps the whale warm in frigid seas.
3. Starbuck and Stubb cut the scarf line into the blubber.
4. The attendees, sharks and sea vultures, make a funeral banquet of the whale.
5. The head makes up one-third of the whale.
6. The head is as silent as the ancient Sphinx.
7. Captain Mayhew does not want to spread the epidemic that plagues his ship.
8. The men both fear and revere Gabriel. They told their captain that they would desert the ship if Gabriel were put off it.
9. Moby Dick's fluke knocked him out of the boat.
10. Gabriel believed Moby Dick to be his Shaker god.

Suggested Essay Topics
1. Summarize the gam with the *Jeroboam*. What new interpretation of Moby Dick does this encounter offer? How does the story of Macey support Ahab's interpretation? What elements make this episode foreboding?
2. Describe the butchering of the whale. What becomes of the head? Why does Ishmael compare the head to the Sphinx? What does Ahab say to the head? Explain the allusions he makes.

Chapters LXXII – LXXVIII

Summary

During the process of stripping the blubber from the whale, Queequeg must mount the carcass to secure the hook. For safety, he is attached to a monkey rope, a line which runs up the side of the ship and is attached to Ishmael.

Ahab orders the killing of a right whale because Fedallah has told him that a boat with a sperm whale head on one side and a right whale head on the other cannot sink.

Stubb and Flask kill a right whale. While they are towing it back to the boat, they discuss Fedallah. Stubb believes him to be the devil and suggests that Ahab has made a pact with him.

Ishmael contrasts the two whale heads now hoisted on either side of the ship. The sperm whale's head is symmetrical, but the right whale's is "inelegant." Ishmael sees the mouth as "really beautiful and chaste-looking."

Within the sperm whale's head is a well of precious spermaceti. Tashtego mounts the main yardarm to lower a bucket into the tun and begin the process of bailing out its 500 gallons of spermaceti. When Tashtego slips and falls into the head, the whole thing falls from the side of the ship. Queequeg jumps into the water, swims to the sinking head, cuts a hole in it, reaches in, and pulls out Tashtego.

Analysis

The theme of the unity of man is symbolized by the line that connects Queequeg and Ishmael. Furthermore, the line symbolizes the interrelatedness of all human actions. What one man does affects another, and as in the case of Ishmael and Queequeg, it could be a matter of life and death.

Although there is some humor in Stubb's speculation about Fedallah being the devil, it is clearly established that he is an evil presence. Stubb jokes about how Fedallah hides his devil's tail and how his one tooth is shaped like the head of a snake, but when Ahab steps on deck to view the whale head, Fedallah literally stands in Ahab's shadow. Figuratively, Fedallah is Ahab's shadow self.

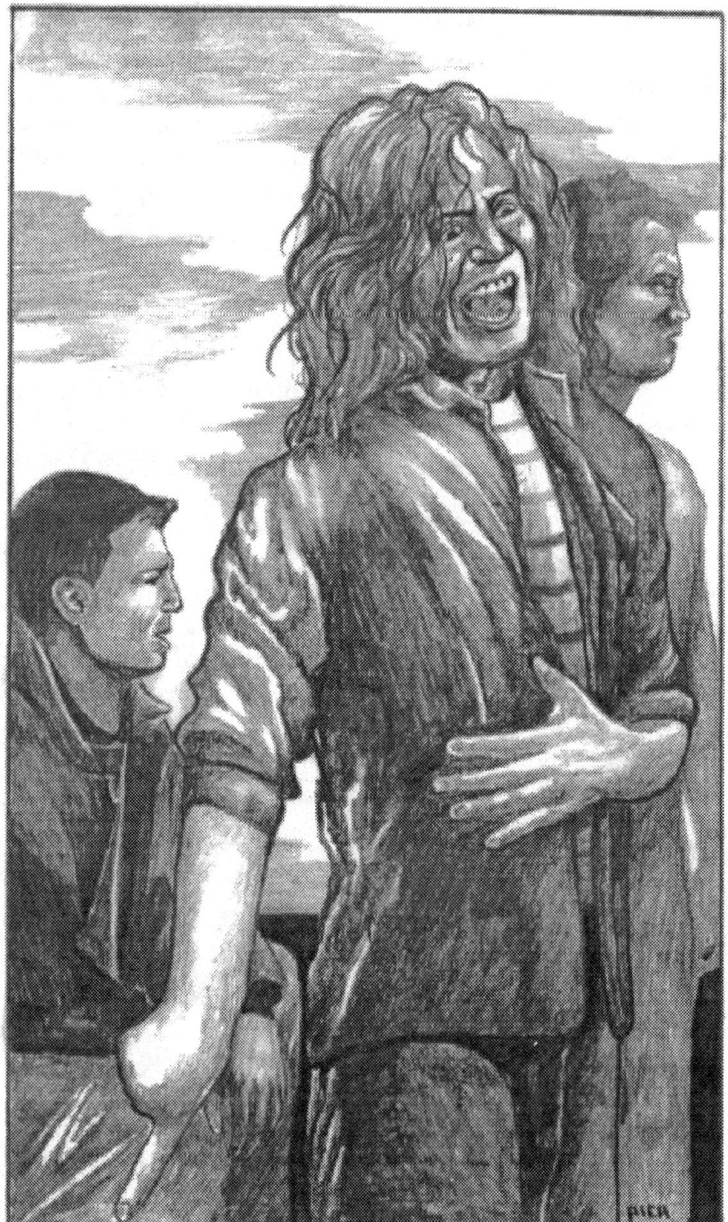

Chapters LXXII-LXXVIII

Part of Ishmael's metaphoric journey toward understanding involves the resolution of dichotomous ideas. With an eye on either side of his head, the whale, can perceive two images at the same time. For man it is not so easy. Like Ahab, man tends to see things as all evil or all good. The two whale heads symbolize the true dualistic nature of the universe.

Study Questions

1. What is the function of the monkey rope?
2. To whom is it attached?
3. Why were the men surprised that Ahab wanted them to hunt a right whale?
4. What was his reason?
5. How does Ishmael interpret the expressions on the whales?
6. To what does Ishmael compare the sperm whale's forehead?
7. What was Tashtego doing when he fell into the head?
8. How was he saved and by whom?
9. To what was his release from the head compared?
10. If Tashtego had died, why would it have been a very "precious perishing"?

Answers

1. The rope is a safety line for the man who stands on the carcass to attach the blubber hook.
2. Queequeg is attached to the end on the whale; Ishmael is attached to the end on deck.
3. The right whale is not valuable.
4. Fedallah told him a ship with a right whale head on one side and a sperm whale head on the other will not sink.
5. The sperm whale's expression shows his indifference to death. The right whale's shows his "practical resolution."
6. The sperm whale's forehead is like a battering ram.

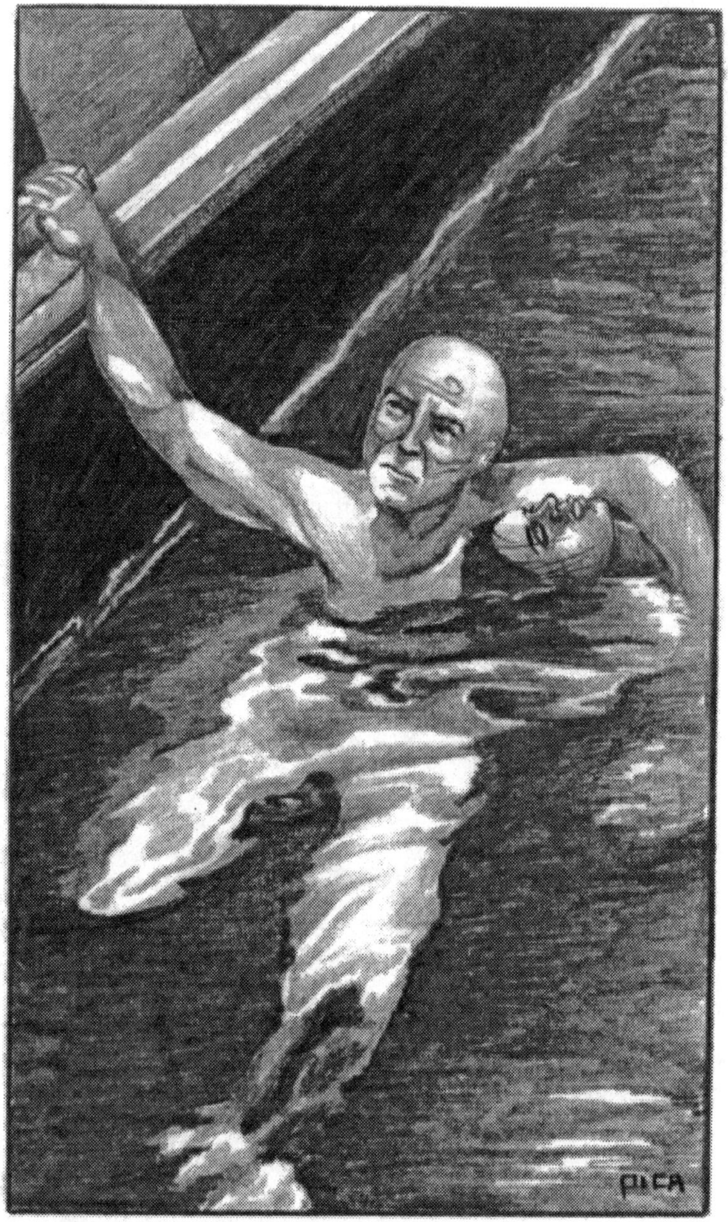
PICA

7. Tashtego was up on a yardarm lowering a bucket down into the part of the head containing the spermaceti.
8. Queequeg dived in the water, cut a hole in the head, and pulled him out.
9. Queequeg pulled him out as if he were delivering a baby.
10. Tashtego would have drowned in the precious, fragrant spermaceti.

Suggested Essay Topics
1. What do the episodes involving the whale heads contribute to character development? In your essay discuss Queequeg, Ishmael, and Ahab.
2. Analyze and discuss what these episodes contribute to the theme. Consider the unity and interdependence of man as well as the duality of the universe.

Chapters LXXIX – LXXXI

New Characters:

Derrick De Deer: *captain of the* Jungfrau

Jungfrau (Virgin): *German ship empty of whale oil*

Summary

Ishmael describes the physiognomy of the whale. The sperm whale has no nose, which gives the creature an added grandeur. Its brow gives it a "high and mighty God-like dignity." The sperm whale is a fit object for pagan worship.

The brain is encased in a skull, which when scaled down, is not unlike man's. The whale's hump rises over one of its largest vertebrae. This hump indicates the "indomitableness" of the sperm whale.

The next whale hunt, involving both the *Jungfrau* and the *Pequod*, illustrates such indomitableness. The *Jungfrau* has no oil, and Captain Derrick De Deer approaches the *Pequod* with the idea of getting some lamp oil from her. However, just as his boat comes near, a pod of whales is spotted.

One blind, crippled old bull struggles along at the rear of the pod. Derrick's four boats and the *Pequod's* three compete to capture this large whale. Queequeg, Tashtego, and Daggoo harpoon the whale first. The whale is killed and secured to the *Pequod*, but the whale begins to sink, pulling the *Pequod* over sideways. Queequeg manages to cut through the fluke chains, and the whale sinks.

Derrick and his men chase after a finback, mistaking it for a sperm whale. The finback is an uncapturable species because of his speed and agility.

Analysis

Once again, Ishmael expresses his appreciation of the great beauty of the whale. He sees similarities between this creature and man, suggesting the unity of man and nature.

Remarking on the inscrutability of the whale's brow, Ishmael tells us, "I but put that brow before you. Read it if you can." Here, it seems Melville tells his readers that it is up to them to find their own meaning in Moby Dick.

Ishmael's diction in recounting the killing of the old whale arouses sympathy. The whale's "tormented" jet, his "agony of fright," his "cruel wound" and "more than sufferable anguish" are "most pitiable." The brute is compared to a bird with a clipped wing, but the bird can express its fear; the whale has no voice. Even Starbuck tries to stop Flask from causing the creature further pain.

The *Jungfrau* is no match for the experienced crew of the *Pequod*. *Jungfrau* means virgin, and so it is appropriate that she is a "clean" ship, "that is, an empty one." Her name also suggests the inexperience of her crew, who go chasing after the uncapturable finback. "Many are the Fin-Backs, and many are the Derricks, my friend," says Ishmael.

Study Questions

1. What gives the whale's physiognomy added grandeur?
2. What does the whale's hump cover?

3. What does Derrick want from the *Pequod*?
4. What does he know about the White Whale?
5. Why does the old whale swim with such difficulty?
6. Who harpooned the whale?
7. What did Starbuck try to stop Flask from doing?
8. What was found embedded in the old whale?
9. What unusual thing happened to the dead whale?
10. Why is the finback an uncapturable whale?

Answers
1. The whale has no nose.
2. The hump covers its largest vertebra.
3. Derrick wants lamp oil.
4. He knows nothing about Moby Dick.
5. The whale is missing his right fin.
6. Queequeg, Tashtego, and Daggoo all harpooned the whale.
7. Starbuck tried to stop Flask from sticking his lance in an ulcerous mass on the whale and causing it more pain.
8. An entire harpoon and a lance-head made of stone were found embedded in the whale's flesh.
9. The dead whale sank.
10. The finback's powerful swimming makes it uncapturable.

Suggested Essay Topics
1. Discuss how pity is aroused for the old bull whale. What is it about his physical appearance that is pitiable? How do diction and figures of speech create sympathy for the creature? In the end, how does the whale prove to be indomitable?
2. What is the meaning of the German word *Jungfrau*? Why is

it an appropriate name for this ship? What does her captain know of Moby Dick? What behavior shows her captain and crew to be inexperienced?

Chapters LXXXII – LXXXVI

Summary

Ishmael names "demi-gods, heroes, and prophets" who have been whalers: among them, Perseus, St. George, Hercules, Vishnu, and Jonah.

Not long after the *Jungfrau* episode, whales are spotted. The chase requires the use of the pitchpole, a 10- to 12-foot lance much lighter than a harpoon. The pitchpole can be thrown some distance to pierce the whale and then pulled back by a line and thrown again and again. Tashtego plants his iron in a whale, but the whale continues its fleet flight. The pitchpole is used to slow it down, and then it is caught.

Ishmael continues his speculations about the whale's physiology. He tells us he is writing this particular passage on December 16, 1851. The topic is the whale's spout through which it breathes. When the whale surfaces, he "breathes," filling vessels on either side of his spine and along his ribs with oxygenated blood. He draws upon this supply when he swims underwater. Although there is no definite answer to the question of whether the spout is vapor or vapor mixed with water, Ishmael maintains it is a kind of mist. Whalemen believe the jet to be poisonous, harmful to the skin, and blinding.

The sperm whale's tail is 20 feet across and its upper surface is at least 50 square feet. Although the tail is incredibly powerful, it is nonetheless very graceful. The whale uses it for progression, hitting, sweeping, lobtailing, and peaking.

Analysis

Whalemen constitute a brotherhood not only of common whalers, but also of the high and the mighty. The whalers Ishmael mentions represent a cross section of cultures. Perseus is a Greek hero and Hercules, a Greek god. St. George is somewhat facetiously

Chapters LXXXII-LXXXVI 73

included among the whalers and is the patron saint of England. Jonah is Hebrew.

The "grand master" of the fraternity is Vishnu, a Hindu god who in his first incarnation was a whale that rescued the Vedas from the bottom of the sea. Ishmael says, "Give us the divine Vishnoo himself for our Lord." This chapter reinforces the idea that all mankind is represented by the whalers. It also supports the theme of the unity of man.

Ishmael continues to see great beauty and majesty in the whale. The peaking of the whale's flukes is "the grandest sight to be seen in all animated nature. Out of the bottomless profundities, the gigantic tail seems spasmodically snatching at the highest heaven." Ishmael also reiterates the inscrutability of the creature. "Dissect him how I may, ...I know him not, and never will." The whale represents the forces of nature, which are destructive, beautiful, and unfathomable.

Study Questions

1. What lovely maiden did Perseus rescue from Leviathan?
2. How does Ishmael change the story of St. George and the Dragon?
3. What are the Vedas and who retrieved them?
4. What question did the old Sag-Harbor whaleman raise about Jonah's surviving in the whale's belly?
5. For what purpose is a pitchpole used?
6. What is the date of the writing of "The Fountain"?
7. How might a whale spout harm a man?
8. What is the length across a whale's tail?
9. What is meant by "peaking"?
10. What are four other actions of the tail?

Answers

1. Perseus rescued Andromeda.
2. Ishmael says the dragon was a whale and St. George's horse

may have been a large seal or sea horse.
3. The sacred Hindu books were retrieved by Vishnu.
4. How could Jonah have survived in the gastric juices?
5. A pitchpole is used to weaken a harpooned whale that continues to swim very fast and may break free.
6. December 16, 1851 is the date of the writing.
7. The spout burns the skin and blinds the eyes.
8. A whale's tail is 20 feet across
9. Before a whale dives, he "tosses" his flukes and much of his body up into the air.
10. The tail also is used for propulsion, striking enemies, slapping the water, and gently sweeping from side to side.

Suggested Essay Topics
1. Discuss the symbolic meaning of whalemen as presented in this section. What famous whalers does Ishmael mention? What cultures do they represent? What were they seeking?
2. Discuss the symbolic meaning of the whale in this section. What is the usual relationship between man and whale? How does Ishmael see the whale? What do these relationships imply thematically?

Chapters LXXXVII – XCII

New Characters:

Guernseyman: *first mate of the* Rose-Bud

Rose-Bud: *French ship with two rotting whales secured to her*

Summary

Near the straits of Sunda, the *Pequod* is chased by Malaysian pirates whom the *Pequod* is able to outrun. The ship then encounters a huge herd of whales. Mid-chase, the whales become "gallied," disoriented and swimming about in all directions. Queequeg

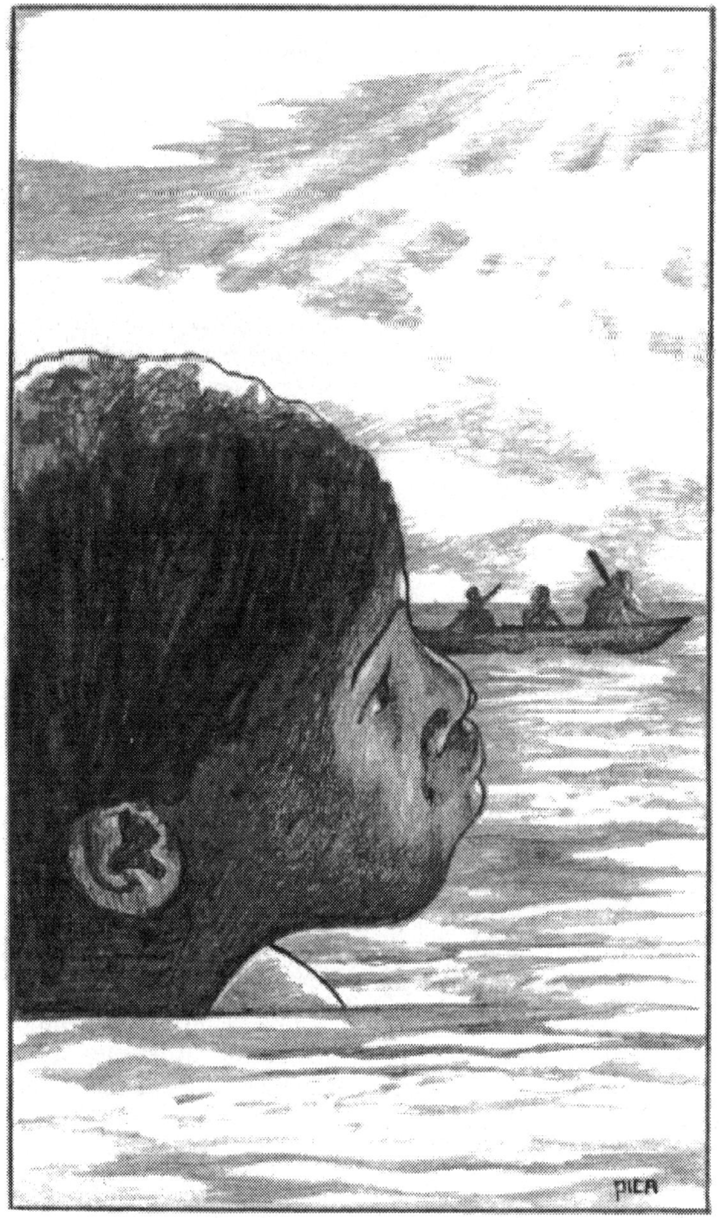
PICA

harpoons a whale that escapes after towing the boat into a calm spot occupied by cows and their calves. The oarsmen pet them. Beneath the surface, cows nurse their young.

The whalers use a "drugg" to injure the gallied whales and slow them down so they can be captured later. A drugged whale, flailing about, invades the calm area and soon the whale boat is pressed on all sides by the whales. In the melee, Queequeg loses his hat. Only one drugged whale is captured.

Enormous herds of whales such as these are sometimes encountered, but schools of whales, consisting of 25 to 50 whales are more frequently seen. These schools usually consist of all males or all females. A female school is accompanied by a schoolmaster, a full-grown male.

In the previous hunt, waif poles were used to mark ownership of whales which had been "drugged." By law, such whales would be considered Fast-Fish. A Fast-Fish is any fish secured to a ship or secured to any implement of that ship such as a waif pole or harpoon.

A curious English law states that the head of a fish belongs to the King, and the tail to the Queen. Nothing is left for the whaler. Ishmael cites a case in which this law has recently been applied in England.

A few weeks after the encounter with the huge herd of whales, the *Pequod* encounters the *Rose-Bud*. On one side of her is a blasted whale, one which has died a natural death and is in some stage of decay. On the other side is a whale which has dried up and died owing to some kind of digestive problem.

Holding his nose all the while, Stubb visits the boat, and discovers they know nothing of Moby Dick. The chief mate, a Guernsey-man, recruits Stubb's help in convincing the captain to cut loose the stinking carcasses. While Stubb insults the captain in English, the chief mate convinces the captain that the rotting whales will cause death and disease on their ship. The captain orders the whales cut loose.

Stubb knows the dried up whale contains valuable ambergris. Ambergris is a fragrant yellow, waxy substance used in perfumes. Stubb and his men are able to get several handfuls of the stuff before Ahab calls them aboard.

Analysis

The irony of the gallied whale scene is that while whalemen slaughter and maim whales, they can at the same time take pleasure in them. Ishmael calls his moments with the cows and their babies "enchanted" and feels secrets of the deep have been revealed to him. The scene also brings together birth and death.

The calm in the center of the gallied whales is symbolic of the soul at peace in the midst of external turmoil. "…while ponderous planets of unwaning woe revolve round me, deep down …I still bathe me in eternal mildness of joy."

The *Rose-Bud* chapter provides a good deal of humor. The name of the stinking ship is, of course, ironic. Stubb's insults of the French and their captain are quick and cutting. Without the captain knowing, Stubb calls him a baboon to his face. Ironically, the captain is so grateful, he offers Stubb a glass of wine. The final irony is that Stubb tricks the Guernsey-man, who tricked the captain.

Study Questions

1. Where does the *Pequod* come upon the huge herd?
2. What is a "drugg"?
3. Where does the harpooned whale tow Ishmael's boat?
4. What truth is there in "the more whales the less fish"?
5. What becomes of a schoolmaster in old age?
6. What is a Fast-Fish?
7. What happened to the whale captured by the Dover fishermen?
8. What is ironic about the name of the *Rose-Bud*?
9. How does the Guernsey-man trick his captain?
10. How does Stubb trick the Guernsey-man?

Answers

1. The *Pequod* encounters the herd near the Straits of Sunda.
2. A drugg is a block of wood attached to a harpoon by a long

line and used to slow down gallied whales.
3. Ishmael's boat is towed into a center of calm.
4. Of all the whales, the *Pequod* captured only one.
5. The schoolmaster, a full-grown male which accompanies a female school, lives in isolation when he grows old.
6. A Fast-Fish is somehow secured to a boat, either directly or by signs of ownership such as a waif pole.
7. The whale was claimed by the Lord Warden for the Duke.
8. The *Rose-Bud* is rank.
9. The Guernsey-man, translating for his captain, pretends that Stubb has witnessed death on ships to which blasted whales are secured.
10. Stubb helps him to convince the captain to cut loose the valuable dried-up whale.

Suggested Essay Topics

1. Describe the calm in the gallied whale scene. What "secrets" were revealed to Ishmael there? Explain fully.
2. What is the tone of chapter XCI? How is this tone established at the outset and maintained throughout the chapter? Who is the central character in this episode? Explain.

Chapters XCIII – XCIX

Summary

Pip replaces an injured man in Stubb's boat. Pip is jarred from the boat and caught in the harpoon line. Tashtego grudgingly cuts the line to save Pip and loses the whale in doing so. On another hunt, Pip is once again thrown into the sea, but this time Stubb leaves him. Pip is later picked up by the *Pequod*, but his experience has left him mad.

Ishmael explains more steps in the processing of the whale. As the sperm cools in the tubs, it hardens. The sailors dip in their hands and squeeze the lumps back to liquid. Also, the whale's phallus is skinned, the skin is dried, arm holes are cut in it, and the mincer slips it on before cutting up pieces of blubber for the melting pots.

The blubber is melted down over a kiln in two try-pots. The sailors often help themselves to the cooled oil to keep their lamps burning even as they sleep. The cooled oil is put in casks and stored below.

Pacing the deck, Ahab, stops to study the doubloon he nailed to the mast. In its symbols, he sees himself. Starbuck interprets it as a symbol of God. Stubb, Flask, the Manxman, Queequeg, Fedallah, and Pip also study and interpret the meaning of the doubloon.

Analysis

"The Castaway" and "The Squeeze of the Hand" are dualistic chapters. In the first, the tender-hearted, jovial Pip, left adrift in the "heartless immensity" of the sea, experiences total isolation. The following chapter deals with the opposite theme, the unity of man. While Ishmael is squeezing the globs of sperm, he also squeezes other men's hands and experiences a reverie of affection and love.

The cult of brotherhood is treated somewhat ironically in "The Cassock." The "apron" worn by the mincer looks like a priest's cassock and is made from the male "grandissimus" of the whale. Ishmael notes that biblical characters have worshipped such idols.

Ishmael is on the helm one night as the fires of the try-works create a hellish scene. At one point, he becomes totally disoriented and a "bewildered feeling as of death" comes over him. On a thematic level, Ishmael has been deceived and led to despair by evil on the *Pequod*, but like a "Catskill eagle," his soul is able to soar up out of the depths to the true light.

The interpretations of the doubloon emphasize once again the ambiguity of meaning. Each man sees something different in the engravings on the coin. Ahab sees himself, the world, and his journey to destruction. Starbuck sees the trinity of God. Stubb sees the life of man. Flask sees only monetary value.

From the engravings, the Manxman predicts when Moby Dick

will be sighted. Queequeg tries to match up the engravings with his tattoos, but sees nothing in the coin of any value. Fedallah, a fire worshipper, bows down to the sun engraved on the coin. To Pip it is the navel of the ship; and once it is taken down, at the first sighting of Moby Dick, the ship and her men will be destroyed.

Study Questions
1. What is a ship-keeper?
2. Why was Pip put into Stubb's boat?
3. Why was Tashtego reluctant to cut the line to save Pip?
4. How was Pip rescued?
5. What was the cause of Ishmael's disorientation?
6. What are the try-works?
7. How is the oil stored?
8. What was on top of each mountain engraved on the coin?
9. What country had minted the doubloon?
10. What would Flask buy if he won the doubloon?

Answers
1. Ship-keepers are the men who handle the ship while the whale boats are out. Pip was usually a ship-keeper.
2. One of Stubb's oarsmen had been injured.
3. Tashtego would lose the whale he had harpooned.
4. The *Pequod* picked up Pip.
5. Ishmael, half asleep, had turned around toward the stern.
6. The try-works are brick kilns used to melt down the blubber.
7. The oil is put in casks and stored in the hold.
8. On one mountain was fire; on another, a tower; on the third, a crowing cock.
9. The doubloon was from Ecuador.

10. Flask would buy 1,660 cigars.

Suggested Essay Topics

1. Describe the engravings on the doubloon. Explain how Ahab, Starbuck, Stubb, Flask, Fedallah, and Pip interpret the meaning of the coin. What is revealed about each character through his interpretation?

2. What is the atmosphere of "The Try-Works?" Analyze the images that create this atmosphere? What happens to Ishmael during this scene? Explain the final image of the Catskill eagle.

Chapters C – CV

New Characters:

Captain Boomer: *one-armed captain of the* Samuel Enderby

Dr. Bunger: *ship's doctor aboard the* Samuel Enderby

Samuel Enderby: *hospitable English ship*

Summary

The *Pequod* has a gam with the Samuel Enderby. The blubber-hook is lowered for Ahab to be hoisted aboard the English ship. Captain Boomer lost his arm to Moby Dick. His boat was smashed and his arm pierced by a loose harpoon. Later, his arm had to be amputated. His carpenter made him a whale-bone arm.

Captain Boomer tells Ahab he has seen the White Whale, but advises him to let well enough alone. Ahab becomes so agitated that Dr. Bunger approaches him to help, but Ahab pushes him against the bulwarks and hurriedly leaves.

The *Samuel Enderby* was named after the man who brought the first whaler into the South Pacific. Ishmael had the opportunity to board the English ship many years after the *Pequod*'s voyage. He remarks about her wonderful hospitality.

Ishmael has become somewhat knowledgeable about whale skeletons by dissecting a cub sperm whale and by inspecting the skeleton of a stranded whale on a Pacific island that he was visiting. The skeleton had been turned into a shrine. By Ishmael's calculations, the skeleton of a large sperm whale is between 85 and 90 feet long.

Fossil whales show that over the centuries whales have grown in size. Ishmael believes that whales will never become extinct.

Analysis

Captain Boomer and Ahab are exact opposites. Boomer sees Moby Dick as "a noble great whale" and wisely advises Ahab, "He's best let alone." To Ahab, the whale is a "magnet."

When Boomer tells the story of his mishap, Ahab interprets Moby Dick's actions as a conscious attempt to free the whale Boomer had harpooned. Boomer replies, "How it was exactly, I do not know." Dr. Bunger says that what is taken for malice in Moby Dick is actually awkwardness. Ahab sees Moby Dick as the incarnation of evil; to Boomer, the whale is a noble creature, but nothing more than a whale.

The two ships also provide contrast. The *Pequod*, with her pagan crew and mad captain, is the exact opposite of the *Samuel Enderby* whose captain and crew enjoy a camaraderie which they extend to their visitors. Ishmael himself attests to the spirit of that jolly ship.

In discussing the magnitude of the whale, Ishmael comments on the magnitude of his book. To write it, he needs a condor's quill to dip into Vesuvius' crater. The hyperbole suggests the "out-reaching comprehensiveness" of his narrative. "To produce a mighty book, you must choose a mighty theme."

Study Questions

1. What problem had Ahab not anticipated in the gam with the *Samuel Enderby*?
2. How is that problem solved?
3. Describe how the two captains greet each other.
4. Describe the relationship between Boomer and Bunger.
5. What does Ahab do to Bunger? Why?

Chapters C-CV

6. What is the Enderby Whaling House famous for?
7. When did Ishmael go aboard the *Enderby*?
8. How does Ishmael know about whale skeletons?
9. What had the natives on the Arsacidean island made of the whale skeleton?
10. What does Ishmael think about the extinction of whales?

Answers

1. Ahab hadn't thought about the difficulty he would have boarding the other ship.
2. He was hoisted aboard on a blubber-hook.
3. The captains cross their whale-bone limbs.
4. Boomer and Bunger have a caring relationship.
5. Ahab pushes Bunger when the doctor tries to calm him.
6. The Enderby Whaling House opened up the South Sea and Japanese whaling grounds.
7. Ishmael spent time on the *Enderby* many years after his voyage on the *Pequod*.
8. Ishmael had dissected a small whale and measured the skeleton of a beached whale.
9. The skeleton was their temple and god.
10. Whales will survive eternally.

Suggested Essay Topics

1. Compare Captain Ahab and Captain Boomer. Consider their appearances, their experiences, their relationships with their crew, and their ideas concerning Moby Dick.
2. What does Ishmael learn from his study of whale skeletons? What does he learn on the Arsacidean island of Pupella? Why does Ishmael admit the futility of studying whale skeletons to understand the whale?

Chapters CVI – CIX

Summary

Ahab had left the *Samuel Enderby* in such haste that he did damage to his ivory leg. Prior to the *Pequod*'s voyage, he had had another mishap involving his leg. Ahab had been found unconscious, lying face down, the leg nearly piercing his groin. The wound had not totally healed when the *Pequod* sailed, which explains why Ahab kept to his cabin at the beginning of the voyage. Because Ahab is now wary of any weakness in his leg, the ship's carpenter fashions him another.

A leak is suspected in the oil barrels. Starbuck enters Ahab's cabin to ask permission to "up Burtons";—that is, to take the barrels out of the hold and find the leak. Ahab forbids it, for this requires the ship to heave to for a week or more, something Ahab is loathe to do. The two men argue and Ahab points a loaded musket at Starbuck. Starbuck does not flinch and says, "Ahab beware of Ahab; beware of thyself, old man." Later, after some thought, Ahab reverses his decision and orders the barrels hoisted.

Analysis

To Ahab, the mishaps involving his leg make perfect sense, for he believes that misery begets misery. The gods themselves are not happy and "the sad birthmark in the brow of man is but the stamp of sorrow in the signer." Ahab believes the universe to be malevolent, and his ivory leg is a symbol of that sad fact.

Ahab's discussion with the carpenter is of interest for both its structure and its content. Melville again breaks the narrative prose, this time by inserting a section of interior monologue. In it, the carpenter discusses the relative merits of an ivory leg. This section is followed by a dialogue between the carpenter and Ahab.

Ahab tells the carpenter that he would like the blacksmith to fashion a man as Prometheus did, but Ahab would like the man to be 50 feet tall, heartless, and with a brain the size of a quarter acre. This man would look inward; the top of his head would have a skylight to give him the illumination to do so.

Although Ahab values self-knowledge, he fails to see a connection between self and universe. In fact, as we have previously seen, he believes self and universe to be at odds. "Cursed be that mortal interindebtedness," Ahab says. Furthermore, Ahab appears to value intellect over emotion. It is ironic that he is expressing this to a man who has been described as very skillful, but remarkably unintellectual.

In the cabin scene, Starbuck dares to stand up to Ahab, but not to defy him. Both agree that what they came "20,000 miles to get is worth saving"; but Starbuck means the oil, and Ahab means his revenge on Moby Dick. Cleverly, Ahab decides to give in on the barrels issue because he knows if anyone were to lead a mutiny, it would be Starbuck. Ahab does not want to cause "disaffection in the important chief officer" at this point.

Study Questions

1. Why did Ahab need a new leg?
2. Before going on the voyage, how had Ahab been injured?
3. What mystery does this incident solve?
4. What are some of the skills of the ship's carpenter?
5. What does Ishmael suggest happened to the carpenter's brains?
6. Why would Ahab want his ideal man to have a skylight?
7. On what matter does Starbuck go to see Ahab in his cabin?
8. What answer does Ahab give Starbuck?
9. How does Ahab threaten Starbuck?
10. What warning does Starbuck give Ahab?

Answers

1. When Ahab hurriedly left the *Samuel Enderby*, he damaged his leg.
2. Ahab had fallen and the splintered leg had wounded him.
3. Ahab stayed in his cabin at the beginning of the voyage to recover from this wound.
4. The ship's carpenter pulls teeth, makes soothing ointments,

and crafts earrings from shark bone.
5. The carpenter's brains must have oozed into his fingers.
6. The skylight allows for self-illumination.
7. The barrels are leaking in the hold.
8. Ahab tells Starbuck not to hoist the barrels.
9. Ahab aims his loaded musket at Starbuck.
10. Starbuck tells Ahab that he, Ahab, will cause his own destruction. "Ahab beware of Ahab."

Suggested Essay Topics

1. What does Ahab's leg symbolize? Of what is it a constant reminder? What does it symbolize to Ahab? Why? How is it a danger to him, both literally and figuratively?

2. Describe the carpenter and the style of the chapters in which he is presented. What is unusual about the narrative technique? What is the tone of these chapters? Why is the structure of the scene between Ahab and the carpenter appropriate? How are these men opposites? How are they alike?

Chapters CX – CXIV

New Characters:

Perth: *the Pequod's blacksmith*

Summary

Working in the dank hold to hoist the barrels, Queequeg becomes sick and nearly dies with fever. He orders the carpenter to make "a canoe" such as those in which the fallen whalemen of Nantucket are laid to rest. In the coffin, Queequeg places the iron from his harpoon, biscuits, water, and a bag of earth. He climbs in it, crosses his arms, and asks to have Yojo placed on his breast.

Pip asks Queequeg when he goes on his journey to seek out one called Pip, who has long been missing, and give him comfort.

Chapters CX-CXIV 87

Queequeg, however, recovers when he remembers he has some duty to take care of on shore. He makes a sea chest of his coffin and on its lid, carves patterns corresponding to his tattoos.

As the *Pequod* sails into the Pacific, Perth, the blacksmith, prepares the tools for the whale hunting that will ensue. Perth is an unhappy old man who lost his family because of his drinking.

Ahab asks Perth to forge him a special harpoon. The iron of the harpoon is made of the nailstubs from the shoes of race horses. Ahab himself forges the shank. The barbs, made from razors, are tempered not in water, but in the blood of Tashtego, Queequeg, and Daggoo.

Analysis

The theme of death is explored in this section. Ishmael sees the "immortal health" of the soul in the eyes of his dying friend. He imagines that a dying man experiences revelations. Queequeg himself envisions death as a sailing away to the stars, which his people believe to be islands.

Pip feels the shame of his cowardly "death" and compares it to Queequeg's "game" death. He beats a dirge for Queequeg on his tambourine. In an apostrophe to death, Ishmael cries, "Oh, Death, why canst thou not be timely?" If Perth had died a timely death, his family would have been spared. Ahab, who recognizes a kinship in Perth, asks him how he can endure life and advises him to go mad.

That death is a focus of these chapters is appropriate since the *Pequod* is coming closer to her fateful encounter with Moby Dick. Ahab prepares for this encounter by tempering his harpoon in pagan blood and baptizing it not in the name of God, but "in nomine diaboli."

Study Questions

1. What causes Queequeg's illness?
2. What does he put in his coffin?
3. How does Queequeg explain his recovery?
4. What does he do with his coffin?

Chapters CX-CXIV

5. What caused the deaths of Perth's wife and children?
6. What does Ahab want Perth to make for him?
7. What are the iron and barbs made of?
8. What seam does Ahab ask Perth to smooth?
9. In what are the barbs of the harpoon tempered?
10. What temporarily soothes even Ahab?

Answers

1. Working in the slimy, damp hold causes Queequeg's illness.
2. Queequeg puts the iron of his harpoon, biscuits, water, dirt, and Yojo in his coffin.
3. Queequeg recovered to take care of some unfinished business.
4. Queequeg turns the coffin into a sea chest and carves its lid with designs like his tattoos.
5. Because of his alcoholism, Perth could not support his family and they died.
6. Ahab wants Perth to make a harpoon with which he will kill Moby Dick.
7. The iron is made from horseshoe nails and the barbs from razors.
8. Ahab asks Perth if he can smooth the seams of his brow, which are etched to the depth of his skull.
9. The barbs are tempered in blood.
10. The tranquility of the Pacific soothes even Ahab.

Suggested Essay Topics

1. How is the theme of death developed in this section? How does Ishmael view death? What are his theories regarding the soul? What will finally be revealed to us in death? What is the "final harbor" to which he refers in "The Gilder"? What other ideas about death are presented?

2. Compare Ahab and Perth. Describe the scene where Ahab approaches Perth. What makes it seem that Perth understands Ahab and vice versa? In what important ways are they different?

Chapters CXV – CXXI

New Character:

The *Bachelor*: *homoward bound ship full of whale oil*

Summary

Full of oil, the *Bachelor* joyously celebrates the beginning of her homeward journey. The captain tells Ahab he has heard of the White Whale, but doesn't believe in him. He invites Ahab aboard, but Ahab tells him to be on his way.

Soon after, as if the good luck of the *Bachelor* had rubbed off, the *Pequod* kills four whales. Ahab watches as the whale he killed turns its head to the sun, as do all dying sperm whales. Ahab's boat stays with its whale during the night since it is too far from the ship to be brought in before nightfall.

During the night's watch, Fedallah interprets a dream of Ahab's. He predicts that before Ahab dies, Ahab must see two hearses on the sea, one made of American wood and one not made by mortal hands. The Parsee predicts that he will die before Ahab, yet will appear to Ahab after his death. He adds that only hemp can kill Ahab.

Taking the ship's bearings with the quadrant, Ahab in frustration, smashes the instrument and throws it into the sea. He changes course. The *Pequod* is then hit by a typhoon. Her sails are torn to shreds and her rigging glows with corposants, St. Elmo's fire. The three-pronged lightning rods at the top of each of the three masts are aflame. Ahab grabs the lower chain end of the rod to feel the lightning course through him. Starbuck tells Ahab to give up his ill-fated voyage and to head home. Ahab grabs his harpoon—its barbs a forked flame—and drives back his half-mutinous crew.

Ahab orders everything lashed down. The whaleboats are

Chapters CXV-CXXI

drawn up high on their cranes, but Ahab's boat is smashed. Starbuck tells Stubb that the boat is smashed in the stern, exactly where Ahab would stand.

Analysis

The *Bachelor* is the exact opposite of the *Pequod*. Ahab says, "Thou art a full ship and homeward bound, ...call me an empty ship and outward bound." The *Bachelor* is as jolly as the *Pequod* is grim. Ahab considers the captain to be a fool, for he has no depth of understanding concerning Moby Dick. Perhaps this captain can be so happy because he simply chooses not to believe in or even think about Moby Dick and what he may represent.

Ahab claims to have learned a lesson from watching the dying whale turn toward the sun. Though one may try to turn toward the light, it is all in vain; for after death, all efforts are lost. Ahab chooses despair over faith in the light of goodness. "The dark Hindoo half of nature" is more real to Ahab.

Ironically, the Parsee's interpretation of his dream fills Ahab with a sense of immortality, for he believes the predictions impossible. In the next chapter—he throws away the quadrant—to him a symbol of man's limited knowledge, and decides to rely on his own intuition.

His new course brings him into direct conflict with the forces of nature. The ship's rigging glows with St. Elmo's fire and her masts look like candles before an altar. The trinity of flames suggests the Christian trinity, perhaps giving Ahab one last warning. But fire also suggests evil and the forces of destruction, as does the serpent's tongue of flame on Ahab's harpoon. Ahab cries out, "O, thy clear spirit of clear fire, ...I now know that thy right worship is defiance."

Study Questions

1. What are the men of the *Bachelor* celebrating?
2. What does the *Bachelor*'s captain say about Moby Dick?
3. What is in the vial that Ahab takes from his pocket?
4. What curious thing do dying sperm whales do?
5. What will Ahab see before he dies?

6. What is the only thing that can kill him?
7. Why does Ahab smash his quadrant?
8. Why does Stubb sing during the fury of the storm?
9. What happens to Ahab's boat?
10. According to Stubb, why did Ahab remain unharmed when he held the chain end of the lightning rod?

Answers
1. The *Bachelor* is full of oil and homeward bound.
2. The captain says he has heard of Moby Dick, but does not believe in him.
3. The vial contains soil from Nantucket.
4. Dying sperm whales turn their heads to the sun.
5. Ahab will see two hearses, one made of American wood and the other, not made by human hands.
6. Only hemp can kill Ahab.
7. Ahab smashes the quadrant because it tells him only where he is, not where he is going.
8. Stubb sings to bolster his courage.
9. The stern of Ahab's boat is smashed.
10. Stubb says the mast would have to have been struck by lightning before Ahab could have been harmed.

Suggested Essay Topics
1. Analyze the fire symbolism in chapter CXIX. What are the corposants? What did the masts look like as the lightning rods glowed? What did Ahab's harpoon look like? How do the sailors react? How do Stubb, Starbuck, and Ahab interpret the flames?
2. Explain the Parsee's predictions. How does Ahab react? Why? How does the Parsee react when Ahab tramples his quadrant? How is Ahab now determining his course? Explain.

Chapters CXXII – CXXVII

Summary

Starbuck goes below to inform Ahab that the wind has changed to a fair wind. Outside Ahab's cabin, Starbuck removes a loaded musket from the rack. He thinks perhaps he should kill Ahab or at least overpower him and take him prisoner. He reasons that Ahab would have killed him with that very same musket, and Ahab has no compunction about endangering the whole crew. Starbuck turns from the door and sends Stubb back down to tell Ahab about the change in wind direction.

The next morning on deck, Ahab realizes the ship is sailing west, but the compass reads east. The storm had affected the compass needles, a most unsettling omen to the superstitious sailors. To allay their fears and show them his power, Ahab fashions a new compass.

Ahab orders the log and line—another measure of speed and direction—repaired after the line snaps. Pip comes along during the operation and is handled roughly by one of the sailors. Swearing he and Pip will never part, Ahab protects Pip and takes him into his own cabin.

As the ship nears the Equatorial fishing grounds, a man falls from the mast and drowns. The life buoy thrown to him proves to be damaged. The carpenter caulks Queequeg's coffin to make it into a life buoy. Ahab wants it out of his sight.

Analysis

Even though Starbuck knows that Ahab is mad and feels that he will "drag a whole ship's company down to doom," he still cannot kill him. Not only is Starbuck too moral to commit murder, but Ahab's power may be too great for him. Starbuck could not endure the sight of an imprisoned Ahab, who would be "more hideous than a caged tiger." Starbuck feels "alone upon an open sea," a true isolato.

Ahab flaunts his power. Seeing pieces of the smashed quadrant on deck and undaunted by the broken compasses, Ahab boasts that he is "lord over the level loadstone." The only direction the

Pequod now has is whatever Ahab gives it. "In his fiery eyes of scorn and triumph, you then saw Ahab in all his fatal pride." Pride, the classic tragic flaw of *hubris*, will lead Ahab to his downfall.

The ship sails on heedless of ill omens. Ahab is not daunted by the storm, the loss of the instruments, the plaintive cries of the seals, or the death of the first man to look for Moby Dick in the whale's own area.

Ahab does, however, ponder the question of the coffin turning into a life buoy. "What things real are there?" he questions. The coffin has been a canoe, a coffin, a sea chest, and now a life buoy. It is a symbol of the multiplicity of meaning in things and events, a unifying theme of this novel.

Study Questions

1. What information is Starbuck going to report to Ahab?
2. What caused him to think about killing Ahab?
3. Rather than facing Ahab, what does he do?
4. What has happened to the compass?
5. How does Ahab allay the crew's superstitions?
6. What do Ahab and Pip have in common?
7. Whom does Ahab call "creative libertines"?
8. What did the Manxman think the crying of the seals was?
9. What was used to replace the life buoy?
10. What did the carpenter attach to it?

Answers

1. Starbuck is going to report a change in wind direction.
2. The sight of the muskets made Starbuck think about killing Ahab.
3. Starbuck sends Stubb in to Ahab to give the report.
4. The compass was reversed by the storm.
5. Ahab fashions a new compass.

6. Both are mad.
7. Ahab calls the heavens and gods "creative libertines."
8. He thought the crying was caused by drowned men.
9. Queequeg's coffin was made into a new life buoy.
10. The carpenter attached 30 lines to it, one for each crew member.

Suggested Essay Topics

1. Find evidence of Ahab's excessive pride and his defiance of the gods. Before Ahab realizes that his ship is sailing in the wrong direction, what remarks does he address to the sun? What does Starbuck say about Ahab? What does Ahab do about the compass? What are his motives for doing that? What does he say to the broken pieces of the quadrant? Whom does Ahab blame for Pip's condition and how does he express that blame?
2. Discuss all the ill omens in this section. How are they interpreted by the men, by Ahab, and by Ishmael? How does Starbuck see the "fair wind" as an ill omen?

Chapters CXXVIII – CXXXII

New Characters:

Captain Gardiner: *captain of the* Rachel

The *Rachel:* *ship that has lost a whaleboat and its men*

The *Delight:* *ship that lost five men to Moby Dick*

Summary

Captain Gardiner of the *Rachel* begs Ahab's help in finding a whaleboat which was last seen fastened to Moby Dick. In that whaleboat is Gardiner's 12-year-old son. Ahab refuses.

Ahab now spends all his time on deck and refuses to be in Pip's company. Ahab fears Pip will soften his heart and divert him from

Chapters CXXVIII-CXXXII

his purpose. His silent companion on deck is Fedallah, who never takes his eyes off Ahab.

Afraid that his men cannot be trusted to cry out when they see the White Whale, Ahab rigs a basket in which he is hoisted aloft. He entrusts Starbuck with the responsibility of watching the ropes that hold him high above the deck. Only minutes after Ahab has been hoisted up, a black, "savage" sea hawk dives at Ahab's head and takes his hat.

The *Pequod* encounters the *Delight*, which has lost five men to Moby Dick. Her captain is about to bury one of the dead, and Captain Ahab unsuccessfully tries to get the *Pequod* away before the corpse is dropped into the sea.

The "cantankerous thing" in Ahab's soul is temporarily dispelled by a lovely, clear day. Leaning over the side, Ahab drops a tear into the water. He tells Starbuck that he has been at sea for 40 years, leaving behind a young wife and son. He also tells Starbuck to stay on board and save himself when Ahab lowers for Moby Dick. Starbuck futilely begs Ahab to alter his course and head back to Nantucket.

Analysis

In this section, Ahab suppresses the last vestiges of humanity he has. He heartlessly refuses to help Captain Gardiner, a fellow Nantucketer, knowing that he may not be able to forgive himself for such behavior. He refuses to be in Pip's company, for Pip may cure his "malady" and, paradoxically, Ahab's malady is his "most desired health." Even in his intimate conversation with Starbuck, he hardens his heart against thoughts of his wife and son, choosing to blame fate for his actions.

The captain of the *Delight* warns Ahab that "the harpoon is not yet forged" that can kill Moby Dick. Neither this final warning nor the bad omens of the corpse and the sea hawk can turn Ahab from his revenge. He is totally aligned with Fedallah, his dark self. Ahab gazes into the ocean and looks into a reflection of Fedallah's eyes. "…in the Parsee Ahab saw his forethrown shadow, in Ahab the Parsee his abandoned substance."

Ahab's connection to Starbuck with a rope may be compared to Queequeg's connection to Ishmael with the monkey rope. There

Chapters CXXVIII-CXXXII

is a bond between the two men. Ahab trusts Starbuck, and Starbuck recognizes the greatness in his captain. But Ahab is a true isolato who shuns dependency. He speaks to Starbuck of "the desolation of solitude" and the "walled-town of a captain's exclusiveness." His 40 years at sea has isolated him and is symbolic of his refusal to accept the interrelatedness of mankind.

Study Questions
1. How was the *Rachel's* whaleboat lost?
2. With what horrible dilemma was Captain Gardiner faced?
3. What did Stubb think Ahab should do regarding Gardiner's request?
4. Why does Ahab not want to be with Pip?
5. What change has come over the *Pequod*'s crew?
6. Whom does Ahab entrust with the rope attached to the basket in which he is hoisted aloft?
7. What did the bird do to Ahab?
8. What do the sailors of the *Delight* see as the *Pequod* sails away?
9. What family does Ahab have back on Nantucket?
10. What promise did Starbuck's wife make?

Answers
1. The whaleboat had harpooned Moby Dick and was towed by the whale away from the *Rachel*.
2. Gardiner had to decide which son to go in search of.
3. Stubb thought that the *Pequod* should help Gardiner.
4. Ahab is afraid Pip will soften his heart and weaken his resolve.
5. The *Pequod*'s men are gloomy and move about like machines.
6. Ahab gives that responsibility to Starbuck.

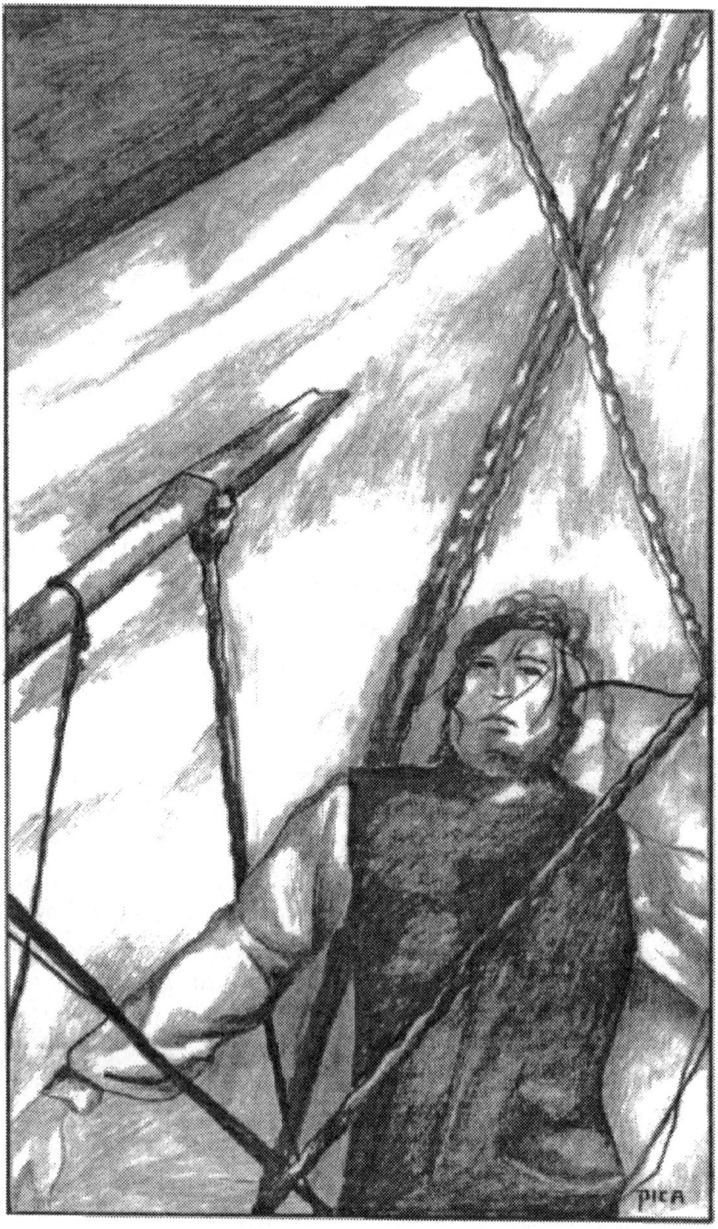
PICA

7. The sea hawk dived at Ahab and took his hat.
8. The sailors see the casket attached to her stern.
9. Ahab has a young wife and son.
10. Starbuck's wife promised to take their son to a hill to watch for his father's return every day.

Suggested Essay Topics:

1. What characters in this section try to turn Ahab from his purpose? Explain fully. What omens serve as warnings to him?
2. Discuss the relationship between Starbuck and Ahab. Why is it ironic that Ahab should trust Starbuck with the rope? Why does Ahab want to look into Starbuck's eyes? What does he see there? Why does the taciturn Ahab open up to Starbuck? What thoughts does he share? What does Starbuck think of Ahab? Why does he turn away in despair?

Chapters CXXXIII – CXXXV and Epilogue

Summary

Ahab is the first to spot Moby Dick. All boat,s except Starbuck's, are lowered and give chase. Just when it seems the whale has sounded, he rises straight up from the deep below Ahab's boat and bites the boat in two. Under Starbuck's command, The *Pequod*, drives the whale off, and Ahab and his crew are rescued.

On the second day, Moby Dick seems intent on destroying all three boats. The harpoon lines, fast to the whale, become so entangled that Stubb's and Flask's boats are drawn into each other and smashed. When Ahab's boat comes to their rescue, Moby Dick lifts it right up out of the water and dumps its men into the sea. Fedallah is drawn under in the tangle of Ahab's line, and Ahab's ivory leg is broken off. Once again the *Pequod* drives the whale away and rescues the men. Starbuck makes one last plea to Ahab to give up the hunt.

On the third day, Moby Dick smashes in the bows of Stubb's

and Flask's boats. When the whale turns, Fedallah is seen lashed by harpoon lines to his flank. The two damaged boats return to the ship to make repairs. When Ahab harpoons Moby Dick, the whale tips his boat. Ishmael falls out, but manages to swim and stay afloat.

The harpoon line snaps as Moby Dick darts through the water and heads straight for the *Pequod*. The whale smashes his forehead into the side of the ship and she sinks. Ahab's boat is the last one left. He once again throws his harpoon and makes fast to Moby Dick. The line runs afoul, and as Ahab stoops to clear it, the line catches him around the neck. He is silently pulled from the boat, down into the depths by Moby Dick.

Ishmael, still swimming, is drawn into the vortex of the sinking *Pequod*. Up from the center of the whirlpool shoots the coffin life buoy. Ishmael, the sole survivor, floats upon the coffin for a night and day until the *Rachel*, still searching for her lost men, rescues him.

Analysis

Once again, Moby Dick is depicted in ambiguous terms. At first sight, the whale is compared to Jove: "...not that great majesty Supreme! did surpass the glorified White Whale as he so divinely swam." He glides on in "enticing calm." Yet it is not long before the whale creates a frenzy of destruction: "Retribution, swift vengeance, eternal malice were in his whole aspect...."

To Starbuck, the whale is a dumb brute simply defending himself. Starbuck pleads with Ahab, "Moby Dick seeks thee not. It is thou, thou, that madly seekest him." It is Ahab that has imbued the creature with evil.

That there is no single meaning that can be ascribed to the whale is central to the understanding of the novel. What Ishmael has learned from his journey is that nothing is absolute, and in all things are a multiplicity of meanings.

Another thing that Ishmael has learned is that, paradoxically, in multiplicity there is unity. That Ishmael survives by floating on Queequeg's coffin reiterates the theme of the brotherhood and interdependence of man. The *Pequod* and her crew symbolize this important concept: "...the one ship that held them all; though it was put together of all contrasting things—oak, and maple, and

Chapters CXXXIII-CXXXV and Epilogue

pine wood" was held together by one long, central keel. Just so "all the individualities of the crew, ...all varieties were welded into oneness."

"The drama's done."

Study Questions

1. What happens to Ahab's boat during the first day?
2. How will the men be rewarded if Ahab sights the whale on the day that the whale is killed?
3. What happens to Ahab on the second day?
4. What happens to Fedallah?
5. When does Ahab see Fedallah again as predicted?
6. What are the two hearses Ahab sees before he dies?
7. How does Ahab die by hemp as predicted?
8. What happens to the *Pequod* and her crew?
9. What "living part of heaven" went down with the ship?
10. How did Ishmael survive?

Answers

1. Moby Dick bites Ahab's boat in two.
2. Ten times the worth of the gold coin will be divided among the crew.
3. Ahab's ivory leg is snapped off.
4. Fedallah is tangled in the lines and towed under.
5. Ahab sees Fedallah lashed to the flank of Moby Dick on the third day of the hunt.
6. The two hearses are Moby Dick and the *Pequod*.
7. A line, made of hemp, catches Ahab around the neck and he is pulled down into the sea by Moby Dick.
8. Moby Dick smashes into the ship and she sinks along with all the crew, except the men in Ahab's boat.

Chapters CXXXIII-CXXXV and Epilogue

9. A sea hawk was brought down with the ship.
10. Ishmael stayed afloat on Queequeg's coffin until the *Rachel* picked him up.

Suggested Essay Topics

1. Discuss the ways in which Ahab and his three mates die. What thoughts and feelings does Starbuck have on the third day? What are Stubb and Flask doing and thinking about as they watch Moby Dick rapidly bearing down on the ship? What is Ahab thinking as he watches his ship sink? What is significant about Ahab's turning his body from the sun?

2. Discuss the ways in which Moby Dick is portrayed in the final three chapters. Cite specific images and incidents. What does this portrayal contribute to the theme? Explain fully.

SECTION THREE

Sample Analytical Paper Topics

Topic #1

Discuss the significance of at least six of the nine gams the *Pequod* has with other ships. Provide a brief description of the gam and then explain its significance.

Outline

I. Thesis Statement: *The gams provide contrast, show varying attitudes to* Moby Dick, *and contribute to major themes.*

II. The *Albatross*
  A. Appearance and name
  B. Theme of alienation

III. The *Town-Ho*
  A. Congenial atmosphere
  B. Attitude toward Moby Dick

IV. The *Jeroboam*
  A. Significance of name
  B. Attitude toward Moby Dick
  C. Theme of alienation

V. The *Samuel Enderby*
  A. Captain Boomer

Sample Analytical Paper Topics

   B. Attitude toward Moby Dick
   C. Theme of alienation
   D. Theme of the unity of man
VI. The *Rachel*
   A. Captain Gardiner
   B. Theme of alienation
   C. Theme of the unity of man
VII. The *Delight*
   A. Appearance and name
   B. Attitude toward Moby Dick
   C. Theme of alienation

Topic #2

Discuss the multiple symbolic meanings of the sea, the coffin, the doubloon, and Moby Dick. Explain the thematic implications of this multiplicity of meaning.

Outline

I. Thesis Statement: *By investing the major symbols of the novel with multiple meanings, Melville suggests that the "phantom of life" is truly "ungraspable."*
II. The sea
   A. Self-knowledge
   B. A benevolent universe
   C. A hostile universe
   D. Isolation
   E. Life
III. The coffin
   A. Death
   B. Life

- C. Unity of man
IV. The doubloon
    - A. Engravings on the coin
    - B. Ahab's interpretation
    - C. Starbuck's interpretation
    - D. Stubb's interpretation
    - E. Flask's interpretation
    - F. The Manxman's interpretation
    - G. Queequeg's interpretation
    - H. Fedallah's interpretation
    - I. Pip's interpretation
V. Moby Dick
    - A. Interpretations of his whiteness
    - B. Gabriel's interpretation
    - C. Ahab's interpretation
    - D. Starbuck's interpretation
    - E. Ishmael's descriptions

Topic #3

Prove that Ahab has many of the characteristics of the classical tragic hero. Explain how Melville imparts heroic qualities to a Nantucket whaling captain. How does Ahab's story evoke both pity and fear? Analyze Ahab's tragic flaw and subsequent downfall.

Outline

I. Thesis statement: *Ahab achieves the stature of a tragic hero, evokes both pity and fear, and suffers a downfall because of his hubris.*

II. Heroic stature
    - A. Biblical allusion to King Ahab

Sample Analytical Paper Topics

    B. Effect of delayed introduction
    C. Bildad and Peleg's description
    D. Ahab's appearance
    E. Elijah's remarks
    F. Ahab's first encounter with Moby Dick
    G. Ahab's power over his men
    H. Ahab during the lightning storm
    I. Ahab's mystic relation with Fedallah

III. Pity
    A. Ahab's loneliness
    B. Ahab's physical injury and suffering
    C. Ahab's intimate conversation with Starbuck

IV. Fear
    A. Association with Fedallah
    B. Tempering his harpoon
    C. Threatening Starbuck
    D. Ahab's madness

V. *Hubris*
    A. Interpretation of engravings on the doubloon
    B. Smashing the quadrant
    C. Making a compass
    D. Ignoring warnings and predictions
    E. Turning his back on the light

VI. Downfall
    A. Ahab's three-day struggle with the White Whale
    B. Ahab's death

SECTION FOUR

Bibliography

Quotations of *Moby-Dick* are taken from the following edition:

Melville, Herman. *Moby-Dick*. Edited by Charles Child Walcutt. Bantam Classic edition. New York: Bantam Books, 1981.

The following works were also cited or consulted:

Ashley, Clifford W. *The Yankee Whaler*. Boston: Houghton Mifflin, 1926. Reprint, New York: Dover Publications, Inc., 1991.

Bloom, Harold, ed. *Modern Critical Interpretations: Moby-Dick*. New York: Chelsea House Publishers, 1986.

"Criticism and Context." In *Moby-Dick* by Herman Melville. edited by Charles Child Walcutt. Bantam Classic edition. New York: Bantam Books, 1981.

McSweeney, Kerry. *Moby-Dick: Ishmael's Mighty Book*. Boston: Twayne Publishers, 1986.

Miller, Edwin Haviland. *Melville*. New York: George Braziller, Inc., 1975.

Introducing...

MAXnotes
REA's Literature Study Guides

MAXnotes™ offer a fresh look at masterpieces of literature, presented in a lively and interesting fashion. **MAXnotes**™ offer the essentials of what you should know about the work, including outlines, explanations and discussions of the plot, character lists, analyses, and historical context. **MAXnotes**™ are designed to help you think independently about literary works by raising various issues and thought-provoking ideas and questions. Written by literary experts who currently teach the subject, **MAXnotes**™ enhance your understanding and enjoyment of the work.

Available **MAXnotes**™ include the following:

Animal Farm	The Great Gatsby	Moby-Dick
Beowulf	Hamlet	1984
Brave New World	Huckleberry Finn	Of Mice and Men
The Canterbury Tales	I Know Why the	The Odyssey
The Catcher in the Rye	Caged Bird Sings	Paradise Lost
The Crucible	The Iliad	Plato's Republic
Death of a Salesman	Julius Caesar	A Raisin in the Sun
Divine Comedy I-Inferno	King Lear	Romeo and Juliet
Gone with the Wind	Les Misérables	The Scarlet Letter
The Grapes of Wrath	Lord of the Flies	A Tale of Two Cities
Great Expectations	Macbeth	To Kill a Mockingbird

RESEARCH & EDUCATION ASSOCIATION
61 Ethel Road W. • Piscataway, New Jersey 08854
Phone: (908) 819-8880

Please send me more information about MAXnotes™.

Name _____

Address _____

City _____ State _____ Zip _____

THE BEST TEST PREPARATION FOR THE
SAT II: Subject Test
WRITING

by the Staff of Research & Education Association

6 Full-Length Exams
- Every question based on the current exams
- The ONLY test preparation book with detailed explanations to every question
- Far more comprehensive than any other test preparation book

Includes a Comprehensive COURSE REVIEW of Writing, emphasizing all major topics found on the exam

REA *Research & Education Association*

Available at your local bookstore or order directly from us by sending in coupon below.

RESEARCH & EDUCATION ASSOCIATION
61 Ethel Road W., Piscataway, New Jersey 08854
Phone: (908) 819-8880

VISA   **MasterCard**

Charge Card Number

☐ Payment enclosed
☐ Visa ☐ Master Card

Expiration Date: ____ / ____
                  Mo   Yr

Please ship REA's **"SAT II: Writing"** @ $13.95 plus $4.00 for shipping.

Name _____

Address _____

City _____ State _____ Zip _____

THE NEW SAT

The Very Best Coaching & Study Course
Completely Up-To-Date for the *New* SAT

SIX Full-Length Practice Tests
with a Diagnostic Test to pinpoint your strong and weak areas

- **Test-Taking Strategies** with study schedule and tips that raise students' scores

- **Verbal Skills Review** covering the vocabulary needed for the new SAT; methods for determining definitions of unfamiliar words; the most frequently tested words; drills to sharpen skills

- **Intensive Practice with Explanations** for Sentence Completions, Analogies, and for the new Critical Reading section

- **Math Skills Review** covering Arithmetic, Algebra, Geometry, and Word Problems; practice drills

- **Intensive Math Practice with Explanations** for the Regular (multiple-choice) Math Section, the Quantitative Comparisons, and the **new** Student-Produced Response section

- **Detailed, easy-to-follow explanations and solutions** to every test question

- Prepared by a team of SAT tutors and test experts thoroughly experienced in the specifics of each particular subject

- Plus...a Guide to Choosing a College, with valuable advice on how to choose and apply to the college of your choice

REA's SAT includes everything you need to score high and build your confidence for the most important test of your academic career

REA *Research & Education Association*

Available at your local bookstore or order directly from us by sending in coupon below.

RESEARCH & EDUCATION ASSOCIATION
61 Ethel Road W., Piscataway, New Jersey 08854
Phone: (908) 819-8880

☐ Payment enclosed
☐ Visa   ☐ Master Card

VISA   **MasterCard**

Charge Card Number

Expiration Date: _____ / _____
                        Mo   Yr

Please ship REA's **"SAT I"** @ $14.95 plus $4.00 for shipping.

Name _____

Address _____

City _____ State _____ Zip _____

REA's Test Preps
The Best in Test Preparation

The REA "Test Preps" are far more comprehensive than any other test series. They contain more tests with much more extensive explanations than others on the market. Each book provides several complete practice exams, based on the most recent tests given in the particular field. Every type of question likely to be given on the exams is included. Each individual test is followed by a complete answer key. **The answers are accompanied by full and detailed explanations.** By studying each test and the explanations which follow, students will become well-prepared for the actual exam.

REA has published over 40 Test Preparation volumes in several series. They include:

Advanced Placement Exams (APs)
Biology
Calculus AB & Calculus BC
Chemistry
Computer Science
English Language & Composition
English Literature & Composition
European History
Government & Politics
Physics
Psychology
United States History

SAT II: Subject Tests
American History
Biology
Chemistry
French
German
Literature
Mathematics Level I, IIC
Physics
Spanish
Writing

Graduate Record Exams (GREs)
Biology
Chemistry
Computer Science
Economics
Engineering
General
History
Literature in English
Mathematics
Physics
Political Science
Psychology

ASVAB - Armed Service Vocational Aptitude Battery

CBEST - California Basic Educational Skills Test

CDL - Commercial Driver's License Exam

CLAST - College Level Academic Skills Test

ELM - Entry Level Mathematics

ExCET - Exam for Certification of Educators in Texas

FE (EIT) - Fundamentals of Engineering Exam

FE Review - Fundamentals of Engineering Review

GED - High School Equivalency Diploma Exam (US & Canadian editions)

GMAT - Graduate Management Admission Test

LSAT - Law School Admission Test

MCAT - Medical College Admission Test

NTE - National Teachers Exam

PSAT - Preliminary Scholastic Assessment Test

SAT I - Reasoning Test

SAT I - Quick Study & Review

TASP - Texas Academic Skills Program

TOEFL - Test of English as a Foreign Language

RESEARCH & EDUCATION ASSOCIATION
61 Ethel Road W. • Piscataway, New Jersey 08854
Phone: (908) 819-8880

Please send me more information about your Test Prep Books

Name _____

Address _____

City _____ State _____ Zip _____